Lecture Notes in Computer Science

Lecture Notes in Computer Science

Edited by G. Goos and J. Hartmanis

414

Antoni Kreczmar
Andrzej Salwicki
Marek Warpechowski

LOGLAN '88 – Report on the Programming Language

With the collaboration of Bolesław Ciesielski,
Marek Lao, Andrzej Litwiniuk, Teresa Przytycka,
Jolanta Warpechowska, Andrzej Szałas,
Danuta Szczepańska-Wasersztrum

Foreword by Hans Langmaack

Springer-Verlag
Berlin Heidelberg New York London Paris Tokyo HongKong

Authors

Antoni Kreczmar
Andrzej Salwicki
Marek Warpechowski
Institute of Informatics, University of Warsaw
PKiN, room 850, P-00901 Warsaw, Poland

CR Subject Classification (1987): D.3.2

ISBN 3-540-52325-1 Springer-Verlag Berlin Heidelberg New York
ISBN 0-387-52325-1 Springer-Verlag New York Berlin Heidelberg

Printing and binding: Druckhaus Beltz, Hemsbach/Bergstr.
2145/3140-543210 – Printed on acid-free paper

Foreword

It is a pleasure for me to comply with the editors' desire to write a Foreword to the report on the object oriented programming language LOGLAN '88 which has been created by the informatics research group of A. Kreczmar and A. Salwicki at Warsaw University. The authors have indeed succeeded in defining and implementing a fully typed programming language of the ALGOL-PASCAL-family where more modern notions like objects, inheritance, processes and communications are harmoniously integrated with more established concepts like block structure, static scoping and higher functionality. The Warsaw group has come up with a characteristic semantical and implementational perception of the notion object which strongly supports LOGLAN's homogeneous language design.

In this foreword, I would prefer not to describe all aspects of this language and compare them with all other existing approaches; this would overcharge me at the moment since object oriented programming is an exploding area. I would prefer to be a companion of our Warsaw colleagues, to say a little about my personal acquaintance with LOGLAN and to address some of its language constructs, their semantics and implementations.

Already in the seventies, the Warsaw group started out from SIMULA 67, a language created in the sixties by O. J. Dahl, B. Myrhaug and K. Nygaard at Oslo University. SIMULA 67 already includes the idea of inheritance, but it is required that inherited classes must have the same module nesting depth as the inheriting ones. The Warsaw people call this phenomenon one level inheritance.

The Norwegians probably had several reasons for this restriction. One predominant reason is: Many level inheritance does not seem to be needed so often in applications. Two further reasons might have been, first, it is rather weary to define a reasonable and natural, i.e. ALGOL-like or static scope semantics for many level inheritance, and second, if one likes to retain Dijkstra's display register implementation technique then registers must be reloaded several times when execution takes place inside the same inheritance chain, e.g. a block, class or procedure body which has been extended by inheritance classes. For one level inheritance this reloading is not necessary; efficient implementation is simple and may follow traditional techniques as demonstrated by SIMULA 67.

But the Warsaw group felt strongly that one level inheritance is too tight a corset. For example, it forces programmers to write unnecessary copies of classes by hand, especially when programs are to be changed or corrected. One level inheritance hinders building up a flexibly usable systems library of classes. The language BETA, another successor of SIMULA 67, which has been defined by researchers at the universities of Aarhus and Oslo independently of the Warsaw group, has many level inheritance too.

So a many level prefixing semantics for LOGLAN has been defined at Warsaw and the known display register implementation technique has been drastically modified such that register reloading in prefix chains is no longer needed.

But there was a price to pay. The semantics was not fully natural, with fully static scope, and it was not invariant against bound renamings. This so-called quasi static scope semantics behaved between static scope as in ALGOL or PASCAL and dynamic scope as in early LISP. Furthermore, the original semantics definition did not fully satisfy aesthetic requirements because of its reference to an implementing machine with a run time stack to store activation records.

These drawbacks have been eliminated in close cooperation with our Warsaw colleagues. We have defined an operational, static scope, ALGOL-like rewrite or copy rule semantics. Rewrite rules for LOGLAN '88 are to be defined not only for procedure and function calls, but also for class generations and block entries. This definition style remains fully at the programming language level without reference to any implementation.

Furthermore, we have observed that static scope semantics does not need to be inefficient. On the contrary, it is much more efficient than quasi static scope semantics with its remaining dynamic scope elements although the latter semantics is oriented at a specific implementation. Quasi static scoping needs as many display registers as there are modules in a LOGLAN program, say μ modules, whereas for static scoping the number of necessary display registers can be bounded by the maximal module nesting depth ν, which is usually much less than μ, and still no reloading inside a prefix chain is demanded.

For implementing BETA, which also adheres to the static scoping philosophy, S. Krogdahl has proposed to construct a code generation optimizer which makes display register reloading for the execution of any inheritance chain more efficient. In the light of Krogdahl's proposal our observation can be formulated in the following manner: reloading can always be optimized in such a way that at most ν registers need to be loaded when an inheritance chain is entered, and reloading is not necessary at all inside a chain. We could never do better because SIMULA and ALGOL need exactly this number ν of registers.

In his dissertation M. Krause has proved the correctness of the novel implementation technique. In addition, A. Kreczmar and M. Warpechowski have come up with a very nice and elegant axiomatic theory on static and dynamic algebras for which LOGLAN '88 programs are models. Both this theory and the new implementation technique are an outflow of considerations about what static scoping really means.

LOGLAN '88 has only mono inheritance and does not provide multiple inheritance as languages like PARAGON, SMALLTALK or ADA do. BETA does not provide multiple inheritance either for the same reasons: an acceptable and consistent semantics and a good implementation technique has still to be found out.

But critics should be fair towards LOGLAN with respect to missing multiple inheritance. Module nesting is another implicit direction of inheritance such that LOGLAN really features two dimensions of inheritance. Both theoretical investigation and existing efficient implementation demonstrate that these two combined inheritance dimensions allow a very clear and satisfying treatment. Other languages have drawbacks also: PARAGON remains with one level inheritance as far as we can see, SMALLTALK has no module nesting, and the language definition of ADA does not allow exploitation of the power of proper inheritance chains although they are available in theory.

I believe that intensive studies of static scoping in object oriented languages will eventually result in appropriate semantics definitions and implementations of languages where multiple and many level inheritance, module nesting and static scoping occur simultaneously. Flat languages without module nesting like SMALLTALK are much better off and can avoid many semantics and implementation problems. But in my eyes, flat programming style should not be the software engineering future. Sure, in connection with module nesting, global output parameters must be treated with great care (sideeffects), but input parameters are much more often needed. And global input parameters are quite harmless and even advantageous. They save much program writing work and their parameter transmissions are more efficient than local parameter transmissions.

Since LOGLAN '88 allows functional arguments for procedures, functions and classes and functional results of functions, this language goes noticably beyond many other practically usable programming languages. LOGLAN '88 has the full power of higher functional programming languages with typing, and the several existing LOGLAN implementations demonstrate that higher functionality does not create serious implementation difficulties, not even in connection with object orientation, coroutines and processes.

Reasonable modern programming languages should allow procedures and functions as arguments. Among other advantages, such parameters and their transmissions represent a simple efficient control mechanism for stack automata activities of arbitrary complexity. We should not forget that without such parameters control has often to be done by expending data manipulation and inquiries.

A most appealing feature of LOGLAN '88 is its incorporation and treatment of processes. SIMULA 67 already has coroutines the syntactical structure and dynamical behaviour of which are somewhat close to processes. So it is reasonable that the Warsaw group has come up with a most elegant and harmonious integration of processes in LOGLAN '88. Processes are objects as classes, procedures, functions and coroutines are. Processes are generated and assigned to appropriate variables similar to classes and coroutines. The authors of LOGLAN have provided synchronous and asynchronous communications by so-called alien procedure calls and send procedure statements, respectively. LOGLAN's alien calls generalize ADA's rendezvous concept which BETA has employed also.

The object oriented programming language LOGLAN '88 which is put forward in this report has been implemented on quite a series of computers and processors, as the authors point out in their preface. LOGLAN '88 is a practically usable programming language. So the informatics community is invited to experiment with this language, especially in the areas of program structuring and communicating processes in order to get further experience, to compare with other approaches and to stimulate discussions of programming language and software engineering concepts.

Kiel, September 1989   Hans Langmaack

CONTENTS

PREFACE

The LOGLAN visiting card

LOGLAN [†] is an object oriented high level programming language born at the Institute of Informatics of Warsaw University. The small team from Warsaw has designed, implemented, corrected, developed, reported, and advertised the language for the last several years.

LOGLAN history

In the mid seventies, the Institute of Informatics at the University of Warsaw initiated the design of a new high level programming language. There were two main inspirations for this research. First, the awareness that the programming language SIMULA-67 was an outstanding contribution to software methodology, and second, that the fast development of multiprocessor hardware would change software practice. We began our work with analytical studies, seminars and lectures dealing with the basic constructs and features of the known programming languages. This helped us to establish the goals a new programming language should reach. By then, however, we decided that the design of a programming language should be a component of a broader software project, called LOGLAN.

There is no doubt that the environment in which our investigations were carried out shed a new light on these goals. In particular, the experience accumulated by a big part of our team in the field of Algorithmic Logic ([1], [19], [20]) influenced the forms of the accepted solutions. The first step of our work was finished in 1977 with the report on the LOGLAN-77 programming language. The report provided a general outline of a universal programming language. Among its most important features let us mention a new approach to modularity and parallel computations ([14]). This version, however, was not implemented. A careful analysis of the constructs suggested in the primary version helped us design an implementation of the language. In the first step of this process we defined the interpreter of LOGLAN in PASCAL for the CDC 6600 computer. At that stage a number of important modifications were proposed, some of them resulted from experiments with the interpreter.

[†] This research was partially supported by the Polish Ministry of National Education Project RP.I.09

The experience of the team in the field of abstract data types and computational complexity helped us to solve one of the most fundamental implementation problems : a proper structure for secure and fast storage management ([4]). In consequence, the language was furnished with a programmed deallocator which allowed the user to control storage resources at run time. The implementation of prefixing at many levels needed a completely new approach. Well-known mechanisms like Dijkstra's display did not allow to abolish SIMULA restrictions (the most important one forbids the use of prefixing at an arbitrary level of a program block structure). Such a solution was found and the users could apply prefixing at an arbitrary program level ([2]).

At the next stage of the research the language, called LOGLAN-82, was implemented for the original Polish two-processor minicomputer MERA 400. The design was modified again in several points because of implementation constraints. After two years of experiments with the compiler of LOGLAN-82 we decided to simplify the language in many aspects and to clarify its syntax. At the same time, it was a good moment to enrich the language with some traditional facilities like enumeration types, static arrays, static records, constant aggregates, etc. consciously omitted in LOGLAN-82.

In 1983 Hans Langmaack from Kiel University observed that the semantics implemented on MERA-400 in some specific situations did not behave according to the so-called static binding rules. This substantial drawback was eliminated due to a certain display register permutation and new display updating algorithms ([11], [12]). In the present version of LOGLAN these algorithms constitute the kernel of proper implementations.

In the meantime the new implementations of LOGLAN-82 were finished. Namely, the versions of Loglan-82 run on VAX 780/VMS, SIEMENS 7760, IBM-PC/XT, PDP11/30/RSX. All of them are available upon request (contact the Institute of Informatics, University of Warsaw).

LOGLAN keystones

LOGLAN belongs to the family of object oriented programming languages (C++ [22], FLAVOURS [13], LOOPS [3], PARAGON [21], SIMULA [5], SMALLTALK [10] etc.). The main constructs for dealing with objects, i.e. classes and inheritance are borrowed from SIMULA-67, but in LOGLAN they are substantially extended. By these extensions the semantics of LOGLAN could not be based on SIMULA-67 semantic principles (the Algol-like way of addressing, stack model of memory management with retention strategy, coroutine sequencing preserving static environment [6], etc.). This concerns especially the addressing algorithms which require more sophisticated methods than simple techniques like Dijkstra's display array and the memory management methods which are different than those used in other object oriented languages. This, we hope, brings new insight into object oriented programming.

On the other hand LOGLAN does not get rid of traditional imperative programming which many object oriented languages do. Primitive types do not need to be objects. Records, static arrays, subtypes and other similar type constructs are admitted. Control structures are traditional and natural. This, we hope, preserves virtues already achieved by imperative programming.

The above two keystones might give the impression that the erected edifice had to be eclectic. We do not share this point of view. Strongly consequent object oriented programming, where all entities are objects, loses its elegance and effectiveness when normal arithmetics come into play. On the other hand the object oriented approach to data types, abstract data structures, coroutine sequencing, parallelism etc. solves many methodological and semantic problems. Why not combine these ideas? This is LOGLAN's main area of defiance.

LOGLAN memory model

One of the main semantic problems of object oriented programming concerns the lifetime of object existence. Pure procedural languages, like ALGOL-60 ([16]), solved this problem immediately – language accessibility rules allow to store and deallocate objects in LIFO manner, so they are stack-implementable. However it is the substantial semantic property of object oriented languages that they are not stack-implementable. In fact, dynamically generated objects are named (in procedural languages they are anonymous), and may be used as long as they are dynamically accessible. There is no easy way to define object accessibility. Practically only a system which can analyze the whole structure of objects may detect non-accessible ones. The problem is exactly the same as in LISP , i.e. how to detect objects which are not accessible and what to do with them since they litter up memory. Hence some object oriented languages transfer this problem to LISP implementation ([10]).

SIMULA implementation was not based on LISP (at the time LISP was not as ubiquitous as today) and was closer to the ALGOL-like model ([5]). In SIMULA memory model objects are pushed on a stack and kept until a garbage collector is triggered and detects non-accessible ones. Then a compactifier squeezes the stack updating simultaneously all references to objects. In some special cases objects in SIMULA may be popped from stack. This is a substantial advantage of the SIMULA model, since on-line deallocation of useless objects makes the system more efficient.

LOGLAN has a different model of memory management from the SIMULA and LISP based object oriented programming languages. The LOGLAN memory model is homogeneous (like in SIMULA), keeps anonymous and named objects in one memory pool. Moreover named objects in LOGLAN may be deallocated not only because they become non-accessible, but also by a programmer's decision. The operation that deallocates a named object and simultaneously releases a memory frame used by it is well known from imperative programming (in PASCAL this operation is called **dispose** cf. [18]). However this operation suffers from a very dangerous disease called *dangling reference*. Dangling reference denotes the situation when a deallocated object is still accessible (this can happen when more than one variable refer to the same object). This evidently can lead to the misinterpretation of program semantics which in the case of an object programming language could be disastrous.

In order to avoid *dangling reference* the LOGLAN memory model has a virtual addressing system. All objects are addressed via an auxiliary address table which eliminates the danger of dangling reference. This way of addressing is secure and sufficiently efficient (each access requires one additional basic operation and a virtual address is one information longer than a direct address). Moreover the LOGLAN memory model supports not only the proper programmed deallocation technique. Due to the elimination of dangling reference we can strengthen the power of inheritance, extend coroutine sequencing, precise parallelism in the way based on object oriented programming and ease many other constructs impossible in SIMULA or a LISP-like model.

LOGLAN peculiarities

Parallelism in LOGLAN has an object oriented nature. Processes are treated like objects of classes. Hence they may be dynamically generated and dynamically deallocated when no longer useful. This provides good facilities for non-system concurrent programming. Communication between processes is provided by alien calls which is similar to remote calls ([7]).

It is particular in LOGLAN that aside from of real parallelism it preserves possibilities for quasi-parallelism given already in SIMULA by means of coroutines. Hence coroutines in LOGLAN cooperate with processes. When a programming system needs to arrange control in a multiplexing manner then it is better to use coroutines - they are more natural and efficient. This is especially useful for simulation problems, but not only. Real parallelism is supported by processes which can be implemented in a shared or a distributed model.

Procedures and functions have full play in LOGLAN. Formal procedures and functions which have been disregarded in many contemporary programming languages are preserved, as in ALGOL. Even more, object oriented philosophy with the LOGLAN memory model helps to widen the applicability of procedures and functions. They can be treated as objects and therefore the language admits to operate on variables having procedures and functions as values. This gives nearly the same expressive power as functional programming.

Aside from normal static arrays LOGLAN provides dynamic adjustable arrays. They are treated as objects, so they are dynamically generated and their index range is defined by a statement, not by a declaration. Moreover these dynamic arrays may be explicitly deallocated. Multidimensional dynamic arrays are constructed as data structures defined in terms of objects.

Exception handling is also embedded in the object oriented environment. Signals raised in exceptional situations are handled by anonymous objects generated like procedures. These objects are the objects of handlers which respond to raised signals. The handler execution can end with the continuation of a normal program execution (like in the case of a procedure) or with the termination of the whole sequence of objects corresponding to the history of a program execution.

LOGLAN inheritance

Inheritance makes object oriented philosophy more valuable. It is a way of building up hierarchies of structures. In SIMULA this mechanism was called prefixing, because of the admitted syntax. However nowadays almost all object oriented programming languages use the term inheritance.

Originally it was a technique akin to macro definitions. When a number of class definitions has a common part it is natural to avoid textual duplications. This was the first step toward inheritance rule. But macro definitions have many drawbacks and one original sin. Namely when a part of the program text is recopied its new occurrence may have inconsistent or misleading semantics. This concerns the identifier binding rules in particular (i.e. the way the applied occurrences of identifiers are bound with the corresponding defining ones). SIMULA defines the semantics of inheritance in terms of object concatenation. If class B inherits class A then in the place where a class B object is generated the proper concatenation of class A and class B object is generated. Object concatenation is a semantic leverage that enables to define the proper semantics of inheritance and some simple addressing algorithms corresponding to static identifier binding rules.

The object concatenation method defined in SIMULA restricts inheritance to one level, i.e. when class B inherits class A both must belong to the same level of module nesting. This restriction made it possible to reduce the SIMULA semantic model to the ALGOL semantic model (with the use of object concatenation). The principles of this reduction are based on the fact that the syntactical environments of concatenated objects are the same (class A and class B have the same syntactical visibility scope).

The problem of inheritance becomes far from trivial when the inherited class A has different level than the inheriting class B. In fact, when a class A object is concatenated with a class B object, their syntactical environments may be different. This is called a multi-level inheritance. The LOGLAN semantic model provides multi-level inheritance. This step forward does not seem to be so important when one only looks at the syntactic structure of a program. However multi-level inheritance has a lot of important semantic consequences. It gives possibilities for free use of inheritance in combination with free use of nesting. Nesting as used in traditional imperative programming permits module subordination (i.e. the outer module may coordinate the way the inner modules should work). Nesting is still very useful in object oriented programming. Now we want to have inheritance rule as a method for defining class hierarchies. SIMULA makes it possible to build up class hierarchies inside each module independently. LOGLAN gives all the possibilities for building up these hierarchies which have subparts from different modules.

Some object oriented languages also provide a construct called multiple-inheritance ([3], [13]). Single-inheritance has a rule that a class may inherit only one class and that there are no cycles in the inheritance relation (e.g. a class may not inherit itself). Hence the inheritance relation in this case has a tree structure. Multiple-inheritance makes it possible to inherit more than one class simultaneously. For instance, class D may inherit classes B and C, while classes B and C inherit class A. Due to this the inheritance relation may have a directed acyclic graph structure.

LOGLAN does not provide multiple-inheritance. This is because such a construct may have different semantic models, each of them creating completely different semantic consequences. For example, the concatenation of objects defined by classes A, B, C, D as above may duplicate an object of class A because it is inherited by B and C independently, or may share one object of class A between classes B and C because there is no reason for such a duplication. Moreover the structure of type consistency becomes very unclear. It is not evident whether the type defined by class B should be consistent with the type defined by class C (they may be consistent because they are inherited by class D). We found some substantial methodological arguments for shared definition of multiple-inheritance, but we found also some substantial methodological argument against this definition. Because of all these semantic questions and, last but not least, because of many implementation impediments, we decided to define the language without multiple-inheritance construct.

ACKNOWLEDGEMENTS

We want to thank all the institutions that helped us financially and/or morally. We give special thanks to Polish Zjednoczenie Mera for a financial grant at an early stage of the project. The implementations of LOGLAN on SIEMENS and VAX were made thanks to the courtesy of Institut für Informatik und Praktische Mathematik of Christian-Albrechts Universität in Kiel and of Istituto di Analisi dei Sistemi ed Informatica del C.N.R. in Rome. We also wish to thank Istituto di Analisi dei Sistemi ed Informatica del C.N.R. for helping us to edit the final version of the report in the TeX environment.

1. Terminology and Notation Rules

The context-free syntactic rules are described using extended BNF. Non-terminal symbols are denoted as sequences of characters enclosed in angle brackets < >, while terminal symbols occur as they stand for themselves. A definition sign will be denoted by ::=, an alternative will be represented by a vertical bar |, as e.g.:

<sign>::= + | −

A sequence of symbols may be bracketed by surrounding it with braces. Such a sequence is optional if it is immediately followed by a question mark. For example, in a rule

<boolean type>::= BOOLEAN { :<expression>}?

the sequence :<expression> is optional. A list of zero or more occurrences of the same sequence of symbols is represented by an asterisk, while a list of one or more occurrences of a sequence of symbols is represented by a plus mark immediately following braces. For example, an identifier, i.e. a sequence of letters, digits and underscores started from a letter, may be defined as follows

<identifier>::= <letter> { _ | <letter> | <digit> }*

A list of the repeated sequence of symbols separated by another sequence of symbols is represented as two sequences, separated by a hash character ♯, as e.g.:

<expression list>::= { <expression> ♯ , }+

denotes a non-empty sequence of expressions separated by commas.

Because of the strong recursiveness of the context-free syntax each section gives, after a number of necessary syntactic rules, some references to other sections. Such a reference has the form S−−>n, where S is a non-terminal symbol and n is a section number. Describing the semantics of the language we shall use the following symbols (with indices if necessary):

A−array	b−boolean
B−boolean expression	c−constant
E−expression	G−statement(or sequence of statements)
i, j, k, n, m−integer	M−unit
N−name	O−object
R−reference value	s−string
S, T−type	x, y, z−real
X−arbitrary identifier	P, Q−process
H−handler	

By an implementation of the language we mean a compiler and a running system. The compiler produces an object code from a source text. This phase is called "compilation time". The object code linked with the running system may run. This phase is called "run time".

The "static" properties of the language are those which concern compilation time. The "dynamic" properties of the language come into play during run time.

An error detected by the compiler makes the program unable to run. Any rule in this report that uses the term "incorrect program", "not allowed', "must" etc., denotes such a situation. Any correct program may run. An error detected by the running system or the hardware suspends normal program execution and causes "signal raising".

In some situations an error may be detected either at compilation or at run time. Such an error will be called static-or-dynamic signal, however the relevant signal will be raised only if the error is detected at run time.

2. Lexical and Textual Structure

The lexical entities are comments, identifiers, reserved words, delimiters, numeric literals, boolean literals, character literals, and string literals.

The basic character set consists of

(a) 26 upper case letters:

A B C D E F G H I J K L M N O P Q R S T U V W X Y Z

(b) 10 digits:

0 1 2 3 4 5 6 7 8 9

(c) 22 auxiliary characters:

. : , ; _ = / + − * < > ' " ( ) # & [ ] { }

(d) the space character and the end of line character

This set can be extended with the following characters:

(e) lower case letters

(f) other special characters, e.g.:

! ? $ @ %

2.1. Comments

Comments have no effect on the meaning of a program and are used solely for program documentation. There are two forms of comments. A comment may be enclosed by braces. In this form a comment may appear between any two lexical entities. A comment may also start with two hyphens and then it is terminated by the end of line. In that form it may only appear following a lexical entity or at the beginning of a line.

Examples:

```
begin   {reserved words are written in boldface lower case}  end
begin  –– another form of a comment
```

2.2. Identifiers

<identifier>::= <letter> { _ | <letter> | <digit> }*

An identifier is composed of letters, digits, and underscores. It must start with a letter and may not be a reserved word (see 2.3).

Identifiers serve for denoting program entities such as constants, variables, types, units and signals. The defining occurrence of an identifier within entity declaration (3.3) defines the meaning of the identifier. All other occurrences of identifiers are called applied and are used to designate declared entities. An entity designated by the applied occurrence of an identifier is defined by binding rules (see 14).

A predefined identifier is an identifier whose meaning is defined in every program without any defining occurrence. Every declaration may either define a new identifier or change the meaning of a defined one.

Examples:

Loglan_source	— lower case letters are allowed;
	— however, in some implementations they may be
	— equivalent to the corresponding upper case ones
PL1	— a digit may appear in an identifier
PL_1	— correct, different from PL1
1start	— incorrect, an identifier cannot start with a digit
Loglan source	— incorrect, space is a separator (see 2.4)
FALSE	— predefined identifier denoting the false value
REAL	— predefined identifier denoting the standard real type

2.3. Reserved Words

There is a certain number of predefined system identifiers which have special significance in the language. They are called reserved words and cannot be declared by the programmer. For better readability of this report the reserved words will be written in boldface lower case; however, in a given implementation they appear in standard upper case. These reserved words are the following:

accept	**disable**			
alien	**do**			**send**
and	**downto**	**if**	**od**	**signal**
andif		**in**	**of**	**step**
		inherits	**or**	
array	**else**	**inner**	**orif**	
arrayof	**enable**	**inout**	**output**	**terminate**
at	**end**	**input**		**text**
attach	**esac**	**is**		**then**
	exceptions		**procedure**	**timeout**
	exit		**process**	**to**
		kill	**put**	**type**
begin	**fi**			
binary	**fileof**	**lastwill**	**raise**	**var**
block	**for**		**random**	
body	**function**	**mod**	**read**	**with**
			readln	**when**
case	**get**	**new**	**record**	**while**
class		**none**	**repeat**	**write**
const		**not**	**return**	**writeln**
copy				
coroutine				**xor**

2.4. Delimiters

A delimiter is either one of the following character from the basic character set

,   ;   =   /   +   −   *   >   <   .   (   )   :   &   [   ]   {   }

or one of the following compound symbols

..   =/=   >=   <=   :=   **   −>

Spaces play the role of separators, i.e. at least one space must separate adjacent and otherwise not separated identifiers (including reserved words) or literals. The end of the line is equivalent to a space as far as its separating properties are concerned.

Brackets [ ] are used in *array bounds* and in indexed names, however in a given implementation they may be replaced by parentheses ( ).

2.5. Numeric Literals

<numeric literal>::= <integer> | <real>
<integer>::= { { <digit> }+ # _ }+
<sign>::= + | −
<real>::= {{<integer>}? . <integer> {E {<sign>}? <integer>}? }
  | { <integer> E {<sign>}? <integer> }

Numeric literals stand for integer and real numbers in the conventional decimal notation. The fractional part of such a decimal representation starts with a point, the decimal exponent starts with the letter E. An isolated underscore character may be inserted between adjacent decimal digits, and it is not significant. Negative numeric literals are not allowed, however a numeric literal with a preceding sign is an arithmetic expression (see 6.2.2).

Examples:

02375	−− integer
2_375	−− integer, the same value as above
35.107E−4	−− real
10007E47	−− real
.002	−− real
−.001	−− it is an arithmetic expression, not a literal

2.6. Boolean Literals

<boolean literal>::=
   # {<base> _ }? {{<extended digit> }+ **#** _ }+ { : <integer> }?
<base>::= 4 | 8 | X
<extended digit>::= <digit> | A | B | C | D | E | F

Boolean literals are used for defining finite sequences of boolean values, where 0 denotes FALSE and 1 denotes TRUE. They start with a hash character **#** followed by a sequence of binary digits.

Sequences of boolean values may be also represented with a base 4, 8 or 16. Then, a digit 4, a digit 8, or a letter X follows a hash character immediately, respectively to the chosen notation. In a hexadecimal notation letters A, B, C, D, E, F have a conventional meaning (from 10 to 15). Thus, an extended digit, i.e. a digit or a letter from A to F, may appear in a boolean literal. For better readability the base is separated from the first digit by an underscore character.

The sequence of binary digits represented in any base may be repeated a number of times. The number of repetitions is defined by an integer numeric literal appearing after a colon.

An isolated underscore character may be inserted between adjacent extended digits, and it is not significant.

The length of a boolean literal is the number of binary digits of the sequence represented.

There are two predefined identifiers FALSE and TRUE denoting the corresponding sequences of length 1.

Examples:

#010101010110	−− length=12
#0101_0101_0110	−− the same sequence as above
FALSE	−− #0
TRUE	−− #1
#X_FFFF	−− #1111_1111_1111_1111 (length=16)
#8_7777	−− #111_111_111_111
#4_3333	−− #11_11_11_11
#0:250	−− the sequence of 250 bits equal 0
#X_ABCD:2	−− #1010_1011_1100_1101_1010_1011_1100_1101

2.7. Character Literals

<character literal>::= ' <character> '

A character literal represents an individual character. It is formed by enclosing a character between single quote characters.

Examples:

```
'a'    -- a
''''   -- '
```

2.8. String Literals

<string literal>::= " {<character>}* "

String literals represent finite sequences of arbitrary characters. They are inserted between quotation marks ". Inside a string literal quotation marks repeated twice "" represent a single quotation mark which does not force the end of a string. The length of a string literal is the length of the sequence represented.

Examples:

```
"again"    -- again
""""""     -- "
""         -- empty string (length=0)
```

3. Units

3.1. Program Units

A program is composed of one or more units. Within any program unit new program entities, i.e. variables, constants, types, signals and other program units may be introduced and applied.

There are six kinds of units : *blocks* (see 13), *procedures* (see 10), *functions* (see 10), *classes* (see 11), *coroutines* (see 15) and *processes* (see 16). *Procedures* and *functions* are called subprograms. *Coroutines* and *processes* are special cases of *classes*. Hence, further on in this report, by a *class* we shall mean (if not stated otherwise) a *coroutine* or a *process* as well.

Units may be nested one inside another with the consequences well-known in any block structured language. Moreover units may be extended with the use of inheritance (see 12). Unit nesting and inheritance are the strongest structuring features of the language. They may freely cooperate in a program giving the user a possibility of designing abstract data types, extensible packages, hierarchical data types, library units, etc.

A unit may consist of two parts - a unit specification and a unit body (see 3.2 and 8). Local entities of a unit may be declared in a unit specification or in a unit body, however its executive part must be contained within a body. This executive part defines unit instance execution (see 3.4).

3.2. Unit Declaration

<unit declaration>::= { {<complete unit> |
  <separate specification>|<continued unit declaration>} };
<complete unit>::= <unit specification> <unit body>
<unit specification>::= **unit** <unit identifier>: <unit head> ; <declarative part>
<unit identifier>::= <identifier>

References:

<separate specification> --> 8.2, <continued unit declaration> --> 8.2
<unit body> --> 8.1, <unit head> --> 8.1
<declarative part> --> 3.3, <identifier> --> 2.2

All kinds of units except blocks (see 13) must be declared. A unit declaration is built of
two parts: a unit specification and a unit body (see 8). A unit specification is a public
part while a unit body is a private part of a unit. Both parts may be provided together in
the form of a complete unit or a unit specification may be textually separated from a unit
body (see 8.2). For classes also a partial specification may be separated from a body. In
either case the remaining part of a unit is called a continued unit declaration.

Examples:

```
unit Euclid: function (n, m:INTEGER):INTEGER;    -- unit head
var k:INTEGER;                                   -- declarative part
begin                                            -- begin of executive part
    do
        k:=n mod m;
        if k=0 then RESULT:=m; return fi;
        n:=m; m:=k;
    od;
end Euclid;                                       -- end of unit body

unit Push_down: class (size: INTEGER);           -- begin of unit specification
var top: INTEGER; STACK: arrayof INTEGER;
. . .                                            -- end of unit specification
begin                                            -- begin of unit body
    STACK := new array [1..size];
    top := 1;
end Push_down;                                    -- end of unit body
```

3.3. Local Entities and the Declarative Part

<declarative part>::= { <declaration> }*
<declaration>::= <unit declaration>| <type declaration>|
  <variable declaration>| <constant declaration>|
  <signal declaration>| <exceptions declaration>
References:
<unit declaration> --> 3.2, <type declaration> --> 4
<variable declaration> --> 5.1, <constant declaration> --> 5.2
<signal declaration> --> 17.1.1, <exceptions declaration> --> 17.1.2

Every new entity introduced in a program must be declared. Entities are declared in declarative parts and in parameter lists (see 9). An entity is local in a unit in which it is declared.

Every declaration (except the *exceptions declaration*) contains the defining occurrence of an identifier. This identifier is associated with the entity being declared. The association of identifiers with local entities declared within one unit must be one to one, i.e. it must define a unique identifier for each entity. Note, that the same identifier may be associated with different entities through declarations in declarative parts of different units.

All non-defining occurrences of identifiers are called applied. The meaning of such occurrences is defined by identifier binding rules (see 14).

Usually there is only one declarative part for each unit. If a user wants to protect some *class entities*, then a *class body* construction (see 8) may be used. In this situation there may be up to three declarative parts for one class.

Declarations of units, variables and signals may appear in any order in the declarative part of a unit. In particular, a subprogram may be called within a declarative part textually before its defining occurrence appears. For the declaration order of types consult 4, of constants consult 5, and of *exceptions* consult 17.1.2.

Examples:

```
    unit Nothing: procedure ;
        unit g: procedure (n:INTEGER);
          begin
            if n>0 then f(n−1) fi
        end;
        unit f: procedure (n:INTEGER);
          begin
            if n>0 then g(n−1) fi
        end;
      end Nothing;
```

3.4. Unit Instances

A unit is a syntactic pattern according to which unit instances are generated at run time. An instance is generated by a subprogram call statement (10.2), a *class generator* (4.5.1.2) or a *block statement* (13). Each newly generated instance of the given unit is different from all the other already generated. Thus during a program execution many different instances of the same unit may be generated.

When an instance is generated, a memory area indispensable for its local variables and parameters is allocated. (It may also include some additional fields for implementation purposes.) If this action fails because of memory overflow, then the signal Mem_Error (see 17.3) is raised.

If a unit is parameterized, the positional correspondence between formal and actual parameters is established. Then the actual parameters are computed and initial transmission for *input* and *inout parameters* takes place (see 9). However, the language does not define the order of actual parameters computation nor the moment of memory allocation, i.e. whether it is done before or after parameters computation.

Local entities of an instance correspond to all entities declared or specified in its pattern unit. The local reference variables in a newly generated instance are initialized by default to **none** (see 4.5), and the initial default values of other variables remain undefined.

When a new instance is generated and the computation of actual parameters is finished, the computation of the currently executed instance is suspended and this newly generated one starts to be executed. For a unit which does not inherit another unit its instance execution starts with the first statement of its executive part. The instance execution of a unit with non-empty inheritance part is defined in 12.

When the sequence of statements of an instance ends or a *return statement* is encountered, the termination of an instance takes place (the termination of a coroutine and a process is defined in another way, see 15, 16). The final parameter transmission is performed, i.e. for *output* and *inout parameters* (see 9). After these actions the unit instance becomes terminated and the execution of the instance which generated the terminated one is continued.

The execution of a program consists of the execution of unit instances.

4. Types

<type declaration>::= **type** {<type identifier> : <type definition> ; }+
<type identifier>::= <identifier>
<type definition>::= <type> | <type name> | **copy** <type name>
<type name>::= <name>
<type >::= <primitive type> | <discrete type>| <composite type> |
   <file type> | <reference type> | <subprogram type>
References:
<identifier> --> 2.2, <name> --> 6.1, <primitive type> --> 4.1
<discrete type> --> 4.2, <composite type> --> 4.3
<file type> --> 4.4, <reference type> --> 4.5
<subprogram type> --> 4.6

A *type* determines a set of values and a family of operations and relations applicable to the elements of this set. Each variable, constant and function used in a program must have a type. This type is specified at the place where the entity is declared.

Types may be named as other program entities. A type identifier is introduced in a *type declaration*.

Some specific properties of types, called type attributes, are predefined. They are denoted by dotted names (see 6.1.3). Some type attributes may be declared by the user, but only in the case of *class types* (see 4.5.1.1). These user defined attributes are denoted also by dotted names (see 6.1.3), and may designate constants, types or signals declared in a class.

The order of *type declarations* in a declarative part of a unit is arbitrary, however it must not lead to a mutually recursive definition (unless a class used as a type is involved in this recursion).

Examples:

    type T: **arrayof** T1;   — an example of a mutual recursive definition
        T1: **arrayof** T;   — which leads to type non-definability;
                    — **arrayof** is an adjustable array, see 4.5.2.

The following example describes the structure of a tree with nodes of an arbitrary degree. Types *node* and *links* are defined in a mutually recursive way. This is legal because *node* is a *class type*.

```
unit node:
class (key: INTEGER);
     var subtrees: links;
end node;
type links: arrayof node;
```

Type definition defines a type in a *type declaration* and in other declarations, e.g. in a variable or in a *function declaration*. This definition may be done either by a *type name*, by an explicit *type definition* or by a copy of a *type name*. *Class type* may be introduced only in the form of a unit declaration (see 4.5.1, 11).

A *type name* (6.1) must designate a declared type. An explicit *type definition* denotes a new type. Each explicit *type definition* denotes a different type, except primitive types (see 4.1) and *adjustable array types* (see 4.5.2). A copy of a *type name* denotes a new type which is a duplicate of a type designated by the *type name*. This new type has identical properties as the original type, however the set of values is disjoint with the set of values of the original type. The copy of a *subprogram type* is not allowed.

A *type declaration* associates an identifier with a *type definition*. This new type is considered to be a local entity of the unit in which it is declared. If a *type declaration* defines a type by a *type name*, then the defined type is the same as the named one.

Class type may be specified only in the form of a *type name*. If this *type name* is a dotted name (6.1.3), then it may be treated only as a *class type*, not as a *class unit*. On the other hand, if this *type name* is a simple name (6.1.1) or a binding name (6.1.4), then it may be treated as a *class type* and as a *class unit* as well (see 11).

Examples:

```
type T : array [1..100] of INTEGER;      -- type declaration
     T1: array [1..100] of INTEGER;      -- type T1 different from T
     T2: T;                              -- type T2 the same as T
     T3: copy T;                         -- type T3 is different from type T
var  i: INTEGER;                         -- specification by primitive type
     A: T;                               -- type specified by a type name T
     j: INTEGER;                         -- i,j are of the same type
     B: T;                               -- A and B are of the same type
     C: array [1..100] of INTEGER;       -- A and C are of different type
     D: T2;                              -- A and D are of the same type
     z: unit complex: class ( re, im: REAL);  -- incorrect, specification by
           end complex;                  -- a class definition is not allowed
```

```
unit Pack: class ;
    unit elem: class ; . . . end elem;
    var Pc: Pack;
        . . .
    block
        var elem: INTEGER;
        type P1: Pack'elem;    -- P1 denotes both type and unit
                               -- elem declared in Pack, see 6.1.4.
             P2: Pack.elem;    -- P2 is only type name and this type
                               -- is equal to P1, i.e. elem in Pack
             P3: Pc.elem;      -- incorrect, Pc.elem is not a type name
                               -- because Pc is not a class name
        var E1: P1;            -- P1 used as a type
            E2: P2;            -- the same as E2: P1
        begin
            E1:= new P2;       -- incorrect, P2 is not a unit name
            E1:= new P1;       -- correct, P1 is a unit name
            E2:= new P1;       -- correct, E2 is of type P1
    end
end Pack;
```

4.1. Primitive Types

<primitive type>::= <numeric type> | <boolean type> |
    <character type> | <string type>
<numeric type>::= <integer type> | <real type>
References:
<integer type> --> 4.1.1, <real type> --> 4.1.2
<boolean type> --> 4.1.3, <character type> --> 4.1.4
<string type> --> 4.1.5

There are few predefined types called primitive, like INTEGER, REAL, etc. The set of values of each of these types may depend on a given implementation. A computer architecture usually gives a fan of possibilities, as for instance, short and long integer arithmetics, single and double precision floating-point arithmetics, and so on. The language provides some tools for making use of these hardware possibilities (see 4.1.1 and 4.1.2).

Numeric types are used for usual integer and real arithmetics. Boolean types are used for operating on the values of two-element boolean algebra as well as on the finite sequences of such boolean values. Character type is used for manipulating the character set, while string type is used for manipulating on the finite set of string literals which are fixed at compilation time.

4.1.1. Integer Types

<integer type>::=INTEGER {: <expression> }? {**raise** <signal identifier> }?

References:

<expression> --> 6.2, <signal identifier> --> 17.1.1

Every integer type is a set of all integers belonging to a specified interval. Such an interval may be specified by an explicit definition of its bounds (see 4.2.2) or by the length of a binary representation of its elements.

For an integer type of the form INTEGER:E, expression E must be a static expression (see 6.2.4) specifying a positive integer constant c. This constant determines a minimum number c of binary digits for the declared integer type. In a given implementation either a built-in hardware integer arithmetic is chosen such that its number of binary digits is not less than c, or alternatively, this integer arithmetic is simulated by the software. In either case, any implementation may have some upper bound for the possible values of c, and so, an attempt to violate this constraint will produce a syntactically incorrect program.

The range of any integer type of the form INTEGER:E must be symmetric around zero, except an extra negative value for the two's complement computers.

The primitive integer types also include the predefined type INTEGER without specification of the constant c. This type stands always for an implementation dependent type which must be a built-in hardware integer type.

Two integer types are the same iff both specify the same number of binary digits and both have the same signal, if any. The sets of values of two integer types are considered equal iff both types specify the same number of binary digits.

Any integer literal represents a value of type INTEGER, unless its type is specified explicitly by a qualification (see 6.3). The set of applicable operations is the following: ABS (the predefined function giving an absolute value), ** (exponentiation), * (multiplication), / (division), **mod** (modulus), + (addition), − (subtraction), + (identity) and − (negation). Some of these operations are partial, i.e. the result of such an operation need not always be well-defined. If, however, such a result is well-defined, then its representation must be correct. For the rules of using integer operations see 6.2.2.

The relations = (equal), =/= (unequal), < (less), <= (less or equal), > (greater), >= (greater or equal) are defined in the natural way (see 6.2.2).

I/O operations (see 18.3) are also applicable to integer types.

Every integer type T has three predefined attributes T.SIZE, T.FIRST and T.LAST. Attribute T.SIZE denotes the number of binary digits chosen by the implementation, while attributes T.FIRST and T.LAST give the minimal and the maximal value in type T, respectively.

In an integer *type declaration* a user may introduce a signal raising (17). For the variables of such a type an attempt to assign an integer value exceeding the range chosen by an implementation will raise the specified signal.

Examples:

```
signal alarm1;
type long_integer : INTEGER:20;
      short_integer : INTEGER:10 raise alarm1;
         c_integer : INTEGER: C;   -- where C is a constant
const C = 30;
var i,j: long_integer;          -- 20 bits of representation
     k: short_integer;
     n: c_integer;
     p: INTEGER;
        . . .
     k:=i*j;                     -- may (but need not)
                                 -- raise signal alarm1
```

4.1.2. Real Types

<real type>::=
  REAL { : <expression> : <expression> }? {raise <signal identifier>}?
References:
<expression> --> 6.2, <signal identifier> --> 17.1.1

Real types provide finite approximations to real numbers. They are always represented as floating point numbers.

For a real type of the form REAL:E1:E2, expressions E1 and E2 must be static expressions (see 6.2.4) specifying positive integer constants c_1 and c_2, respectively. The value of c_1 determines a minimum number of binary digits of binary mantissa, while the value of c_2 determines a minimum number of binary digits of binary exponent. In a given implementation either the corresponding minimum built-in hardware floating point arithmetic is chosen, or alternatively, this arithmetic is simulated by the software. An implementation may have some upper bounds for the possible values of c_1 and c_2, and an attempt to violate this constraint will produce a syntactically incorrect program.

The range of a mantissa as well as of an exponent must be symmetric around zero, except an extra negative value for the two's complement arithmetics.

The primitive real types include also the predefined type REAL without explicit definition of the lengths of mantissa and exponent. This type denotes the predefined by an implementation real type which is always a built-in hardware standard floating point type.

Two real types are the same iff both types specify the same ranges of the mantissa and exponent and both have the same signal, if any. The sets of values of two real types are considered equal iff both types specify the same ranges of the mantissa and the exponent. Any real literal represents a value of type REAL, unless its type is specified explicitly by a qualification (see 6.3).

The operations applicable to real values are the following: ABS (the predefined function giving an absolute value), ** (exponentiation), * (multiplication), / (division), + (addition), − (subtraction), + (identity) and − (negation). Some of these operations are partial. Moreover the result need not be exact and rounding errors may appear. For the strict rules of using real operations see 6.2.2.

The relations = (equal), =/= (unequal), < (less), <= (less or equal), > (greater), >= (greater or equal) are defined in the natural way, however rounding errors may sometimes produce erroneous results.

I/O operations (see 18.3) are also applicable to real types.

Every real type T has two predefined attributes T.SIZE_M and T.SIZE_E. The first one gives the number of binary digits for the mantissa of T, while the latter one gives the number of binary digits for the exponent of T.

In a real *type declaration* the user may introduce a signal raising (17). For the variables of such a type an attempt to assign a real value exceeding the range chosen by an implementation will raise the specified signal.

Examples:

```
signal error1, error2;
type short_real : REAL:10:4 raise error1;
     long_real : REAL:20:8 raise error2;
var x,y: short_real;
    z,t: REAL;
    w: long_real;
    x:=z+t;      —— may (but need not) raise signal error1
```

4.1.3. Boolean Types

<boolean type>::= BOOLEAN {: <expression> }?

References:

<expression> --> 6.2

Boolean types serve for manipulating boolean values (TRUE, FALSE) and finite sequences of boolean values.

The sets of values of two boolean types are equal iff they denote sequences of bits of equal length. In this case two such boolean types denote the same type.

For a BOOLEAN type of the form BOOLEAN:E, expression E must be a static expression (see 6.2.4) specifying a positive integer constant c. This constant determines the length of a sequence of bits. In a given implementation the corresponding minimum built-in hardware boolean arithmetic is chosen, or this boolean arithmetic is simulated by the software. An implementation may have some upper bound for the possible values of c and an attempt to violate this constraint will produce a syntactically incorrect program.

The type BOOLEAN without any expression denotes type BOOLEAN:1.

The operations applicable to the values of boolean types are the following: **not** (logical negation), **and** (conjunction), **or** (inclusive disjunction) and **xor** (exclusive disjunction). Operations **and**, **or** and **xor** are defined only if both arguments are sequences of bits of the same length. In the case of sequences of boolean values all these operations are performed simultaneously on the corresponding positions of the specified sequences.

In addition to these boolean connectives the language provides a concatenation & (see 6.2.3) and an access to an arbitrary bit of such a sequence, i.e. by an indexed name b[i]. The bit components of type BOOLEAN:k are accessible by indexed names (see 6.1.2) in the same way as components of type **array** [0..k−1] **of** BOOLEAN (see 4.3.1).

The relations = (equal) and =/= (unequal) are defined for sequences of equal length in the usual way. The order relation < is defined only for two sequences of bits with the same length and it is the inclusion relation, i.e. a < b iff a and b = a. The other relations <= (less or equal), > (greater) and >= (greater or equal) are defined according to the order <.

I/O operations are also applicable to boolean types (see 18.3).

Every boolean type T has three predefined attributes T.SIZE, T.FIRST and T.LAST. Attribute T.SIZE gives the length of a type T sequence, attribute T.FIRST gives the sequence formed only from 0's and finally attribute T.LAST gives the sequence formed only from 1's.

Examples:

```
type bool1 : BOOLEAN:16;
     bool2 : BOOLEAN:12;
var  b1, bb1 : bool1;
     b2: bool2;
     b3: BOOLEAN;

     b1:=b1 or bb1;
     b1[15]:=TRUE;
     b1:=b1 and (b2 & #X_A);   -- & denotes concatenation
     b3:= b1 <= bb1;           -- correct, b1 and bb1 are of the same type
                               -- and b3 is of type BOOLEAN
     b3:= b1 <= b2;            -- incorrect, b1 and b2 are not of
                               -- the same type
```

4.1.4. The Character Type

<character type>::= CHAR {**raise** <signal identifier> }?
References:
<signal identifier> --> 17.1.1

The predefined type CHAR is a set of all character literals. The order relation < is defined by the given character code. The other relations = (equal), =/= (unequal), <= (less or equal), > (greater), >= (greater or equal) are defined in the usual way.

There is also a predefined function POS from type CHAR into type INTEGER giving the code number of a character value and a predefined partial function CHAR.VAL from type INTEGER into type CHAR giving the character value for the corresponding character code.

If in CHAR.VAL(i) the value of i is outside the range of the code numbers, then a signal is raised (see 17). If the declaration of character type introduces a signal raising, then the specified signal is raised. Otherwise a static-or-dynamic signal Con_Error is raised (see 17.3).

I/O operations are also applicable to character type (see 18.3).

Examples:

```
var u,v: CHAR; i: INTEGER;
const dollar = '$';

u:=dollar;
```

4.1.5. The String Type

<string type>::= STRING

The predefined type STRING serves for manipulating string constants. A string constant is defined either by a constant identifier (see 5.2) or explicitly as a string literal (see 2.8). Any two string (and/or character) constants may be concatenated with the use of operation & (see 6.2.4). The result will be a string constant. The only other operations applicable to the string type are **write, writeln** (see 18.3) and **copy** (see 4.5.3).

A variable of type STRING may have a string constant as a value. The predefined attribute s.SIZE gives the length of a string designated by s.

Examples:

    var s,s1 : STRING;
    const text1 = "nothing " & "else";

        s:=text1;   −− correct (s.SIZE=12)
        s1:=s;   −− correct
        write (s1);   −− correct
        s1:=s&text1;   −− incorrect, s is a variable (not a constant)

4.2. Discrete Types

<discrete type>::= <enumeration type> | <subtype>

References:

<enumeration type> −−> 4.2.1, <subtype> −−> 4.2.2

A discrete type is an ordered set with a finite number of values. Each value of a discrete type has a position number which is an integer number. Position numbers of consecutive discrete values are consecutive integer numbers.

Enumeration types define ordered sets of distinct values. Subtypes allow to bind the range of an enumeration type, a character type or an integer type to a given interval.

4.2.1. Enumeration Types

<enumeration type>::= ({ <enumeration literal> ♯ , }+) {**raise** <signal identifier> }?
<enumeration literal>::= <identifier>
References:
<identifier> −−> 2.2, <signal identifier> −−> 17.1.1

The set of values of an enumeration type is an ordered set of distinct values denoted by identifiers.

The sets of values of two different enumeration types have the empty intersection, even when their values are denoted by the same identifiers.

Order relation < between enumeration literals follows the order of listing. The other relations, i.e. = (equal), =/= (unequal), <= (less or equal), > (greater), >= (greater or equal) are defined in the natural way.

The position number of the first list element is 0; the position number of each other is one more than its predecessor in the list.

The occurrence of an identifier in such a definition is its defining occurrence. The same identifier can appear in different enumeration types within one unit, but such an identifier may be used as a value of one of these types only with an appropriate qualification (see 6.3).

Examples:

> **type** day : (Mon,Tue,Wed,Thu,Fri,Sat,Sun);
> planet : (Mer,Ven,Ear,Mar,Jup,Sat,Ura,Nep,Plu);

> Mon   −− unique
> day(Sat)   −− Saturday
> planet(Sat)   −− Saturn

The language predefines two partial functions applicable to arguments of enumeration types:

> PRED(Q) — for an argument Q of type T the result of the function is the value of type T whose position number is one less than that of Q,

> SUCC(Q) — for an argument Q of type T the result of the function is the value of type T whose position number is one greater than that of Q.

For any enumeration type T there are also three constants predefined as type attributes:

 T.FIRST—the minimum value of type T
 T.LAST—the maximum value of type T
 T.SIZE—the number of elements of type T.

Hence, PRED(T.FIRST) and SUCC(T.LAST) are undefined for any type T, and in such cases a static-or-dynamic system signal Con_Error is raised (see 17.3). In the case when the declaration of type T introduces signal raising, then the specified signal is raised instead (see 17). If no signal is raised, then the following relations are satisfied:

 PRED(SUCC(Q))=Q
 SUCC(PRED(Q))=Q

There is also a predefined function POS from T into type INTEGER:

 POS(Q)– for an argument Q of type T the result of the function is the position number of Q in type T (e.g. POS(T.FIRST) = 0),

and there is predefined type attribute – partial function VAL from type INTEGER into T:

 T.VAL(i) — the argument i must be of integer type; the result of the function is the value of type T whose position number is i. If i is not in the range of the position values of type T, then a static-or-dynamic system signal Con_Error is raised (see 17.3).

If a program is correct and a system signal Con_Error is not raised, then the following relations are satisfied:

 POS(SUCC(Q))=POS(Q)+1
 POS(PRED(Q))=POS(Q)−1
 T.VAL(POS(Q))=Q
 POS(T.VAL(i))=i

Operations *put* and *get* are also applicable to enumeration types (see 18.1, 18.3.2).

Examples:

 POS(Mon)=0
 day.VAL(3)=Thu
 planet.FIRST=Mer
 SUCC(planet(Sat))=Ura
 SUCC(day.VAL(3)) =Fri
 SUCC(day.VAL(10))   −− raises Con_Error

4.2.2. Subtypes

\<subtype\>::= \<bound pair\> {**raise** \<signal identifier\> }?
\<bound pair\>::= \<expression\> .. \<expression\>

References:

\<expression\> −−> 6.2, \<signal identifier\> −−> 17.1.1

A subtype restricts the set of values of an integer type, a character type or an enumeration type without changing the set of applicable operations and relations.

In the definition of a subtype EF..EL expressions EF and EL must be static (see 6.2.4) and their types must be consistent with type INTEGER or with type CHAR, or with any of the enumeration types. They give two values F and L, respectively. The values F and L must satisfy the condition F<=L. The range F..L describes the values from F to L inclusive.

The position number of an integer number in a subtype is the number itself. The position number of a character value in a subtype is its code number (see 4.1.4). The position number of an enumeration value in a subtype of an enumeration type T is the position number of this value in type T.

A type defining the initial ordering of a subtype T is called the base type of T. Thus, the base type of an integer subtype is type INTEGER or another integer type, if explicitly qualified. The base type of any character subtype is type CHAR. The base type of a subtype of an enumeration type T is type T.

For any subtype T, predefined type attributes T.FIRST and T.LAST give the minimum and the maximum value of type T, respectively. Attribute T.SIZE gives the length of representation in case of integer types and the number of elements in case of other discrete types. Since any subtype is a subset of its base type, operations PRED, SUCC and POS (see 4.2.1) are also defined for subtypes. The result of PRED and SUCC may however exceed the range of the subtype.

For a variable of a given subtype T an attempt to assign a discrete value outside its range will raise the specified signal, if present in the declaration of T, otherwise Con_Error is raised.

Examples:

```
type working_day: day(Mon)..day(Sat);
     T : 1..n raise alarm;              -- where n is a constant
     T1: 1..100;                        -- subtype of INTEGER
     T2: long_integer(1000) ..
           long_integer(100_000_000)    -- subtype of long_integer
     near_planet : Mer..Mar;
     digit : '0'..'9';
var d: day;
    d:=SUCC(working_day(Sat));          -- correct, d is of type day
```

4.3. Composite Types

<composite type>::= <static array type> | <record type>
References:
<static array type> --> 4.3.1, <record type> --> 4.3.2

Composite types provide methods for manipulating some groups of variables as single variables and some groups of values as single values.

The sets of values of two different composite types always have the empty intersection.

4.3.1. Static Array Types

<static array type>::=**array** [{ <index range> ♯ , }⁺] **of** <type definition>
<index range>::= <type definition>

References:

<type definition> --> 4

A *static array type* defines a composite type consisting of a number of indexed components of the same type. It determines the structure of a variable and of a value as well. A component of a *static array type* is determined by indices belonging to the specified discrete types. Thus the *type definition* standing for an index range must define a discrete type. The order of indices is significant. For any *static array type* the number of its components and the way of their indexing are fixed at compilation time.

Components of *static array* value or variable are accessible by indexed names (see 6.1.2).

A *static array type* S of the form:

   array [T1, T2,..., Tk] **of** T

where T1, T2,..., Tk are discrete types, denotes a k−dimensional array consisting of components of type T. The i−th index, $1<=i<=k$, ranges over the whole discrete type Ti. Access to a component of S is allowed only if all indices are defined (see 6.1.2).

Examples:

```
type S : 1..100;
     digit: '0'..'9';
     U : array [S,digit] of INTEGER;
     T : array [S] of array [digit] of INTEGER;
var  u: U;
     t: T;
     s: S;
     d: digit;
```

t[s][d]   −− correct
u[s,d]   −− correct
t[s]   −− correct
t[s,d]   −− correct
u[s][d]   −− incorrect
u[s]   −− incorrect

4.3.2. Record Types

<record type>::= **record** { <component list> ∦ ; }⁺ **end** { <type identifier> }?
<component list>::= { <component identifier> ∦ , }⁺ : <type definition>
<component identifier>::= <identifier>

References:

<identifier> --> 2.2, <type definition> --> 4,
<type identifier> --> 4

A *record type* defines a composite value consisting of named components which may be of different types. Each component is introduced by an appearance of its identifier in a component list. Distinct components must have distinct identifiers. A *record type* can be used for defining a structure of a variable or of a value as well.

All components appearing in one component list terminated by a *type definition* are of a specified type. An identifier occurrence in a component list is its defining occurrence. The components of a *record variable* or a *record value* are accessed by applying such identifiers in dotted names (see 6.1.3).

An optional identifier following *end symbol* must match the type identifier associated with the declared record.

Examples:

```
type T : record
            i,j:INTEGER;
            A: array [day] of planet;
         end T;
     U : record
            B: record
                 B1: array [1..n]  of CHAR;
                 B2: T;
               end B;
            bool: BOOLEAN:20;
         end U ;
var  t: T; u:U;
     t.i:=t.j;
     u.B.B1[2] :='A';
```

4.4. File Types

<file category>::= **random** | **text** | **binary**
<file type>::=
  <file category> **fileof** { <type definition> | ({<type definition> ♯ , }*) }

References:

<type definition> ――> 4

The file is a finite sequence of components of the same or of different types.

In the file *type definition* a single type or a sequence of types in parentheses specify the types of components which may be saved on the declared file. For the kinds of types that may appear in a file declaration consult 18.1.

There are three file categories defined by the keywords **text**, **binary** and **random**. The category of a file defines the internal structure of a file and the way a file can be accessed (see 18.1).

During a program execution a variable of *file type* should be associated with an external file. Permanent files are associated by the user and scratch files are associated by default (see 18.2). An external file is a store where file components are located.

Examples:

        type T : **binary fileof** INTEGER;
             T1: **random fileof array** [1..20] **of** CHAR;
             rec : **record**
                     i,j : INTEGER;
                     bool: BOOLEAN;
                   end;
        var   file:T;
               file1:T1;
               file2: **text fileof** (INTEGER, rec);

4.5. Reference Types

<reference type>::= <class type> | <adjustable array type>
<reference literal>::= **none**

References:

<class type> --> 4.5.1, <adjustable array type> --> 4.5.2

A *reference type* is used for designating objects or *adjustable arrays*. An object is an instance of a *class*, a *coroutine* or a *process*. An object may also contain an inheritance sequence of instances (see 12.1). The value of a *reference type* gives a reference to an object or to an *adjustable array*.

An object or an *adjustable array* must be generated in a sequence of statements by a generator (see 4.5.1.2, 4.5.2.2), and then, it may be accessed. Elements of an object will be called object attributes. Elements of an *adjustable array* will be called *array components*. Access to object attributes is achieved via dotted names (see 6.1.3), access to *adjustable array components* is achieved via indexed names (see 6.1.2).

The reference to an object (*adjustable array*) may be the value of many different reference variables. So, if an object attribute changes, all variables containing the reference to this object will give access to the new value of the attribute. The same concerns the access to *adjustable array* components.

A reference value need not always be defined. The reference constant **none** denotes the undefined reference. No object can be referred to by this reference. Access to an attribute (a component) of the undefined reference is, of course, not allowed and in such a case a system signal Acc_Error is raised (see 17.3). The default type of the reference literal **none** is the set of all reference values. This type however may not be used directly in the program.

The relations = (equal) and =/= (unequal) are defined between two reference values of any type. The reference values R1 and R2 satisfy R1=R2 iff both are **none** or both refer the same object (*adjustable array*), otherwise they satisfy R1=/=R2.

4.5.1. Class Types

<class type>::= <type name>
References:
<type name> --> 4

Class is the basic notion of the language. The complete exposition of this notion is presented in 11 and 12. In what follows merely a short introduction to its use as a type is given.

Class types are introduced in the form of a *class unit* declaration (see 11). An identifier associated with such a *class unit* denotes also *class type*. Such a type determines the set of reference values which may refer any object of this class or any object of a class whose inheritance sequence (see 12.1) includes this class.

The copy of a *class type* with the same set of values may be done by a *type declaration* (see 4) in which a *class type* is specified by a *type name* (see 6.1 and 11). The copy of a *class type* with a different set of values may be done by a *copy type declaration* (see 4).

There is also a predefined system type OBJECT. The reference values of this type may refer any object of an arbitrary *class*, *coroutine* or *process*.

Examples:

        unit C : **class** ;   —— here C is the class type
        end C;
        type A: C;   —— type A is the same as type C
               B: **copy** C;   —— type B is a duplicate of type C
                              —— with different set of values

4.5.1.1. Class and Object Attributes

The local entities of a class are introduced in a formal parameter list (see 9.1) or in a declarative part (see 3.3). These local entities may be *class attributes*, like the attributes of other kinds of types, or may also be object attributes.

The values of *class type* attributes are static, while the values of object attributes are dynamic, i.e. they may differ from one object to another. Object attributes of a class are attributes of all objects of this *class type*. If a variable contains the reference to an object, its attributes can be accessed by dotted names (see 6.1.3).

Variables and subprograms which are local entities of a class are object attributes.

Local entities of a class which are constants, types or signals are *class type attributes*.

Classes which are the local entities of a class are simultaneously *class type* attributes and object attributes. But if a class is treated as an object attribute, then it can be used only as a *class unit*, not as a *class type*. On the other hand, if a class is treated as a *class type* attribute, then it can be used only as a *class type*, not as a *class unit*.

Class type attributes are denoted by dotted names (6.1.3) like the attributes of discrete types (4.2).

The predefined system type OBJECT has neither object nor type attributes since there are no attributes which are common to all classes. By this, if an access to an object attributes is made by dotted name with variable of this type then the qualification (see 6.3) of this variable by the proper *reference type* is necessary. *Examples:*

```
    unit complex: class (re,im:REAL);
        var mod: REAL;
        unit add: function (z: complex): complex;
          begin
            RESULT:=new complex(re+z.re,im+z.im)
          end add;
        begin

    mod:=sqrt(re**2+im**2)    -- attributes re, im and mod are applied in
                              -- the sequence of statements of class complex,
                              -- all three are object attributes
    end complex;

    unit node: class (value:INTEGER;   left,right:node);
    end node;

    var z1,z2:complex;
```

```
    v:node; r: REAL;

    r:= z1.re          -- re, mod, add and left are
    r:= z2.mod         -- object attributes accessible
    z1:= z2.add(z1)    -- from outside of the objects
    v:= v.left         -- denoted by z1, z2 and v

unit PACKAGE: class;
    unit F: function (i:INTEGER): INTEGER; ...
    end F;
    const n=300;
    type T : array [1..n] of INTEGER;
    var   a,b:T;
  begin { executive part }
end PACKAGE;
const m= PACKAGE.n+1;   -- PACKAGE.n is a class type attribute
                        -- accessible from outside of class PACKAGE
var A:PACKAGE.T;        -- PACKAGE.T is a class type attribute
                        -- accessible from outside of class PACKAGE
    Pz: PACKAGE;        -- correct, Pz is of type PACKAGE
    Z: OBJECT;          -- correct, Z is of a predefined type OBJECT
    i: INTEGER;

    Pz.a:=Pz.b;         -- here, a and b are object attributes
    Z:=Pz;              -- this assignment is correct
    Z.a:=Z.b            -- these accesses are incorrect because
                        -- type OBJECT has no attributes
    i:=PACKAGE.F(5)     -- incorrect, F is an object attribute
                        -- not a class attribute
    i:=Pz.F(5)          -- correct since F is an object attribute
```

4.5.1.2. The Class Generator

<class generator>::= **new** { <class identifier> | (<dotted name>) }
    <actual parameter list>
References:
<actual parameter list> --> 9, <class identifier> --> 11
<dotted name> --> 6.1.3

The execution of a *class generator* causes the generation of a new *class instance* (see 3.4). This new *class instance* defines a new *class object* (see 4.5.1.1). The reference to this object is the value returned by the *class generator*.

A *class unit* whose object is to be created is designated by a *class identifier* (see 6.1 and 11) or by a dotted name. If it is a dotted name, then it should be enclosed in parentheses.

Examples:
    { Continuing the previous examples }
    $z1$:=**new** complex (1.0,1.0);
    $z2$:=**new** complex (1.0,1.0);
    {
    $z1$ denotes to an object different from $z2$,
    although with the same values of attributes:
    ...
    $z1$=/=$z2$
    $z1$.re=$z2$.re
    $z1$.im=$z2$.im
    $z1$.mod=$z2$.mod
    ...
    A *class generator*:
    new node(1,**new** node(3,**none** ,**none**),**none**);
    produces a tree with two internal nodes 1 and 3
    }
    unit Queue: **class** ;
      unit qelem: **class** (i: INTEGER); ... **end** ;
    ...
    end Queue;
    var Q: Queue;
       el: Queue.qelem;

    Q := **new** Queue;
    el := **new** (Q.qelem) (7)   -- correct, Q.qelem is a dotted name
                                -- being a class unit name

4.5.2. Adjustable Array Types

4.5.2.1. The Adjustable Array Type Declaration

<adjustable array type>::= **arrayof** <type definition>
References:
<type definition> --> 4

Adjustable arrays differ from *static arrays* in many aspects. An *adjustable array* is generated at run time with components indexed by integer values while a *static array* value is simply a composite value whose indexing is fixed at compilation time. The bounds of an *adjustable array* index need not be known at compilation time and they are established at the moment of *array generation* (not declaration).

An *adjustable array type* defines a *reference type* whose value may be a reference to a *one-dimensional array*. Components of this array are variables of the same specified type. They are accessible by indexed names (see 6.1.2) with index values of type INTEGER. Predefined functions LOWER and UPPER of type INTEGER are *adjustable array attributes* defining lower and upper bounds of index range. These attributes are accessible by dotted names like object attributes (see 6.1.3, 4.5.1.1). An *adjustable array* is created by an *array generator* (see 4.5.2.2).

In order to admit multi-dimensional arrays the specified type may be again of the form **arrayof** T. Then a one-dimensional array has, as its components, references to *adjustable arrays*.

Two *adjustable array types*, T1 specified as **arrayof** S1 and T2 specified as **arrayof** S2, are the same iff S1 and S2 designate the same type (see 4). They determine equal sets of values iff types S1 and S2 are semantically equivalent (see 4.7). If types S1 and S2 are not semantically equivalent, then T1 and T2 have disjoint sets of values. The copy of an *adjustable array type* gives the same set of values as the original type. An *undefined adjustable array* is denoted by **none**, as in the case of objects.

Examples:

    type T : **arrayof** REAL; T1: **arrayof** arrayof INTEGER;
    var   t:T; y: T1; z: **arrayof** arrayof REAL;

    z[i]   -- it is a reference value of type **arrayof** REAL
    z[i, j]   -- it is a component of type REAL
    z[i] [j] -- correct, the same as above
    t[i, j]   -- incorrect, too many indices

4.5.2.2. The Array Generator

<array generator>::= **new array** [{ <bound pair> ♯ , }+]
References:
<bound pair> --> 4.2.2

All expressions appearing in bound pairs must be consistent with type INTEGER and are computed at the moment of an *array generation*. An *array generator* of the form:

new array [EL..EU]

may be used only as the right hand side of an assignment statement (see 7.1) or as the actual parameter value assigned to the corresponding formal variable in the *input parameter passing mode* (see 9.1).

An *array generator* creates a new *adjustable array*. The type of this array is defined by the type of the variable which it is assigned to. The reference to this *adjustable array* is returned as the value of the generator. The index of this array ranges from L to U, where L is the value of EL and U is the value of EU, respectively, both computed at the moment of the *array generator* execution. (The values L and U must satisfy the condition L<=U.) The expressions EL and EU need not be static (see 6.2.4), so the index range may be defined dynamically.

An *array generator* of the form:

new array [EL1..EU1, EL2..EU2]

produces a sequence of linked *adjustable arrays*. The generator value is a *one-dimensional adjustable array:*

new array [EL1..EU1]

where each of its component values is a reference to a new *adjustable array* produced by the implicit *array generator* of the form:

new array [EL2..EU2]

For *multi-dimensional array generators* this rule is iterated, however no commitment is made to a particular order of the corresponding implicit *array generators*. Hence, if Mem_Error (see 17.3) is raised it is not defined which of the arrays are already generated and which are not.

Examples:

For the declarations of *adjustable arrays* as in the previous example.

y:=**new** array [1..n, 1..m]   −− n,m need not be constants

{ An example of a triangular array generation: }
z:=**new** array [1..n];
for i:=1 **to** n
do
    z[i]:= **new** array [1..i];
od;

{ For array z created as above the following equalities hold:
z.LOWER=1 z.UPPER=n
z[n].LOWER=1 z[n].UPPER=n
z[i].LOWER=1 (for $1 <= i <= n$)
z[i].UPPER=i (for $1 <= i <= n$)
}

4.5.3. The Copy Operator

<copy operator>::= **copy** (<expression>)

References:

<expression> --> 6.2

The *copy operator* generates a new object (or *adjustable array*) which is a copy of its argument and delivers as a result a reference value referring to this new object (or *adjustable array*). The value of a *copy argument* must be a reference, a string or a *one-dimensional static array*. (The reference value may not refer to a *coroutine* or to a *process*, unless it is terminated).

If an argument of *the copy operator* is a reference value not equal to **none**, it designates O1 — an object (or an *adjustable array*). Then a new object (*adjustable array*) O2 of the type of O1 is implicitly generated with all attributes (components) copied from O1. The reference to the object (*adjustable array*) O2 is returned as the value of *copy operator*. If, however, an argument is the reference value equal to **none**, then no object (*adjustable array*) is generated and **none** is returned as the value of *copy operator*.

If an argument of *copy operator* is a string, then a new *adjustable array* A of type **arrayof** CHAR is generated by the implicit *array generator* in the form of:

new array [1..n]

where n denotes the string length (see 4.1.5). Next the string is copied into A, character by character. The reference to *adjustable array* A is returned as the value of *copy operator*.

If an argument of the *copy operator* is a *one-dimensional static array* of type **array** [S] of T, a new *adjustable array* A is generated by the implicit *array generator* in the form of:

new array [L..U]

where L and U are the positions numbers of S.FIRST and S.LAST, respectively. Next the components of the *static array* are copied to A, one by one. The type of A is **arrayof** T and the reference to *adjustable array* A is returned as the value of *copy operator*.

Examples:

```
copy ("this string")
copy (A)                        -- where A is a one-dimensional static array
copy (new complex(1.0,1.0))
```

4.5.4. The Kill Statement

<kill statement>::= **kill** (<expression>)

References:

<expression> --> 6.2

The *kill statement* allows to make explicit deallocation of an individual object (or *adjustable array*) of any *reference type*. It is in some sense a dual operation the generation of an object (*adjustable array*), i.e. whenever an object (*adjustable array*) is created, storage for its data must be allocated and whenever an object (*adjustable array*) is deallocated the storage it occupies is released.

The value R of expression E given in a *kill statement* must be of a *reference type*. *Kill statement* has the following effect:

(1) If R=**none**, then **kill** (E) is equivalent to an empty statement.

(2) If R is the reference to an object (*adjustable array*) O, then the storage occupied by O is immediately released and may be reclaimed.

(3) If X is a variable containing the reference to an object (or *adjustable array*) O, then its value is set to **none** right after the *kill statement* execution.

The deallocation of a *class object* (except a *coroutine* or a *process object*) is legal only if its *class instance* is terminated (see 4.5.1.2). Otherwise the signal Kill_Error will be raised (see 17.3).

For the deallocation of a *coroutine* see 15.2, of a *process* see 16.4.

Examples:

```
z1:= new complex (1.0,1.0);
z2:=z1;
kill (z1);                -- z1,z2 are set to none

z1.im                     -- raises Acc_Error (see 17.3)
z2.im                     -- raises the same signal
```

4.6. Subprogram Types

<subprogram type>::= <function type> | <procedure type>
<function type>::= **function** <formal parameter list> : <type definition>
<procedure type>::= **procedure** <formal parameter list>

References:

<formal parameter list> --> 9.1, <type definition> --> 4

A subprogram type is used for designating a type of *functions* or *procedures*. Hence the value of a subprogram type is a *function* or a *procedure*.

Constants of a subprogram type are declared by unit declarations (10), not by constant declarations (5.2). The type of this constant is a one-element set containing only this subprogram.

Any declared procedure belongs to the set of values of a *procedure type* if its parameter list may replace the formal parameter list specified in this type (see 9.2). Any declared function belongs to the set of values of a *function type* if, in addition to the above condition, the result type specified by the *function type* may be replaced by the result type of the declared function (see 4.7).

Examples:

```
type P : procedure (proc:P);
     F : function (i:INTEGER;p:P;g:F): INTEGER:10;
unit p1: P;
     begin
       proc(p2);              -- proc is the formal parameter from P
     end p1;

unit p2: procedure (r:P);
     begin
       r(p1);                 -- r is a formal parameter of p2
     end p2;

unit f:F;
     var i: INTEGER;
     begin
       i:=f(10,p2,f);         -- f is applied twice
     end f;
```

4.7. Type Consistency

For any expression its type must be checked as to its consistency with the context, e.g. in assignment statements (see 7.1), parameter transmissions (see 9), evaluation of relational and arithmetic operators (see 6.2.3 and 6.2.2), etc. This requirement is called type consistency and is checked at compilation time.

Two non-reference types are consistent iff the intersection of the sets of their values is nonempty (see 4.1, 4.2, 4.3, 4.4). For subprogram types the notion of type replacement is used instead of type consistency (see 4.6).

Two reference types are consistent iff the intersection of the sets of their values contains more than the undefined value **none** only. For consistency of *class types* inheritance is involved (see 12). Note, that the type of literal **none** is the set of all reference values (see 4.5). Type OBJECT is consistent with any *class type*.

Examples:

```
    type TI1: INTEGER;
         TI2: INTEGER:40;
         TR1: REAL;         -- TI1 and TI2, TR1 and TR2 are consistent
         TR2: REAL:5:59;    -- TI1 and TR1, TI1 and TR2 are inconsistent
    type IS1: 0..20;        -- IS1 and IS2 are consistent, and each of them
         IS2: 10..30;       -- is consistent with type INTEGER
         Digits: 0..9;      -- IS1 and Digits are consistent
                            -- while IS2 and Digits are inconsistent
    type day : (Mon,Tue,Wed,Thu,Fri,Sat,Sun);
         planet : (Mer,Ven,Ear,Mar,Jup,Sat,Ura,Nep,Plu);
    { day(Sat) and planet(Sat) are distinct values, so day and planet are inconsistent }
    type T: . . . {any type}
         SA1: array [1..5] of T;
         SA2: array [1..5] of T;
         SA3: SA1;
    {  SA1, SA2 are inconsistent because two different type definitions have different
       sets of values; SA3 and SA1 are consistent, because SA3 is the same as type SA1,
       see 4 }
         DA1: arrayof T;
         DA2: arrayof T;
    { Types DA1 and DA2 are consistent, because they have identical sets of values,
      see 4.5.2.1 }
```

```
      unit C : class (x:INTEGER); end;    -- types C and C1 define disjoint sets
      unit C1: class (x:INTEGER); end;    -- of values, so they are inconsistent
      unit C2: inherits C class; ... end   -- types C2 and C are consistent
   { The set of values of type C2 is a subset of the set of type C values. So they are
   consistent, see 12 }
```

Aside from the notion of type consistency two additional notions concerning types will be used, namely type replacement and semantic equivalence of types. Both are stronger than type consistency. The first notion comes into play for subprogram types (see 4.6) and for virtual subprograms (see 12.5). The latter one is used for parameter list consistency of signal handlers (see 17.1.2) and continued unit declarations (see 8.2).

Two types are semantically equivalent iff the following conditions hold:

(1) they determine equal sets of values

(2) if one of them associates a signal for exceeding range of its values, then the latter must associate exactly the same signal for this range.

Type T1 may be replaced by type T2 iff one of the following conditions hold:

(1) both determine the same set of values

(2) if both are *class types* (see 12.1) or both are subprogram types (see 4.6), then the set of values of T1 includes the set of values of type T1.

Examples:

Continuing the previous examples
```
            -- Types C and C2 are not semantically equivalent,
            -- but type C may be replaced by C2.
```
{ Any type may be replaced by a type semantically equivalent }
```
            -- Types DA1 and DA2 are semantically equivalent and each of
            -- them may be replaced by another one.
```

type Isub1: 0..20 **signal** alarm;
    Isub2: 0..20 **signal** alarm;

      -- types Isub1 and Isub2 are semantically equivalent
      -- any type from Isub1, Isub2, IS1 may be replaced
      -- by one another
      -- IS1 is semantically equivalent neither to Isub1 nor
      -- to Isub2

      -- type C1 is inconsistent with type C, so it is neither
      -- semantically equivalent nor may it be replaced by C

type P : **procedure** (proc:P);
    F : **function** (i:INTEGER;p:P;g:F): INTEGER:10;
unit proc : P;
begin

    ...

end proc;
unit f: **function** (j:INTEGER;g:P;h:F): INTEGER:10;
begin

    ...

end f;
      -- the subprogram type of procedure proc may replace type P
      -- the subprogram type of function f may replace type F

5. Variables and Constants

5.1. Variable Declarations

<variable declaration>::= **var** { { <specification list> {(=<constant>) } ?} ;}+
<specification list>::=<variable list> : <type definition>
<variable list>::= { <variable identifier> ♯ , }+
<variable identifier>::= <identifier>
References:
<identifier> --> 2.2, <type definition> --> 4
<constant> --> 5.2

A variable must be declared. Its type is fixed at the place of its declaration. The value of a variable may be changed at run time (see 7). The initial default values of variables are undefined except for reference variables whose initial default values are always **none** (see 4.5).

An optional initial value of all variables appearing on the specification list may be defined by a constant consistent with the corresponding *type definition*.

Examples:

    type T: **array** [1..100] **of** digit;

        var x,y,z: **arrayof** BOOLEAN;
            t,u: digit (='0');
            X: node;
            A: T (=T('0':100));

5.2. Constant Declarations and Aggregates

<constant declaration>::= **const** {<constant identifier>= <constant> ;}$^+$
<constant> ::= <expression> | <type identifier><aggregate>
<constant identifier>::= <identifier>
<aggregate> ::= ({ <aggregate element> ♯, }$^+$)
<aggregate element>::=<single aggregate element> | <repeated aggregate element>
<single aggregate element>::= <expression> | <aggregate>
<repeated aggregate element>::= <single aggregate element> : <expression>
References:
<identifier> −−> 2.2, <type identifier> −−> 4
<expression> −−> 6.2

A constant may appear as a literal or it may be declared, and then its type and its value are fixed at the place of its declaration. The type and the value of a constant are settled at compilation time and they cannot be changed at run time. The type of a constant must not be a reference type (except a literal **none**), a file type or a subprogram type.

The value of a declared constant may be defined by an expression or by an aggregate preceded by a *type identifier*. If the expression in a constant declaration is not qualified (see 6.3), this expression must define both the type and the value of the constant. If the expression is qualified, then the type of qualification defines the type of the constant. All expressions appearing in a constant declaration must be static (see 6.2.4).

The order of constant declarations in a declarative part of a unit is arbitrary, however it may not lead to constant non-definability because of a mutual or self recursive declaration.

Aggregates serve for defining composite constants of *record* or *static array types*. One aggregate defines a composite value of a given type. Each component value is specified by a corresponding aggregate element.

A single aggregate element defines either a single value specified by an expression or a composite value specified by an aggregate. A repeated aggregate element is equivalent to the sequence of values specified by the value of the single aggregate element repeated a number of times. In such a case the static expression appearing after a colon must specify a positive integer constant c, and then the number of repetitions is equal to c.

If the type of a constant is a composite type, then an aggregate must define all components of the constant and each aggregate element must be consistent with the type of the corresponding component. In the case of a *multi-dimensional static array* the aggregate elements must be again aggregates defining the corresponding components of the array, and so on. In the case of a record the aggregate elements must define all the components of the record in the order of the component list. If a component of the record is of a composite type, the corresponding aggregate element must be again an aggregate defining the whole composite value, etc.

Examples:

```
type digit : '0'..'9';
const pi = 3.1415926;              -- REAL
      pi_half = pi/2.0;            -- REAL
      n = 100;                     -- INTEGER
      one = digit('1');           -- type digit
      uno = '1';                   -- type CHAR
      con = "term";
      text = "A simple "& con;    -- text is a constant: A simple term
      { for the definition of concatenation & see 4.1.5, 6.2.4 }

type T : array [1..3] of INTEGER;
const table = T(1,2,3);
      summa = table[1]+table[2]+table[3];    -- summa = 6
      tb1 = T(1,tb1[2],tb1[1]);              -- incorrect, tb1[2] undefined

type MATRIX : array [0..2,0..2] of REAL;
const identity= MATRIX ((1.0,0.0,0.0),
                        (0.0,1.0,0.0),
                        (0.0,0.0,1.0) );

type scan : array [state,CHAR] of state;
      state : (comment,identifier,numeric,boolean,char,string,delimiter);
var current_char: CHAR; current_state: state;
const automat=     { here a state transition table may be defined };

type triple : record
                A: array [1..m] of digit;
                B: REAL;
                C: record
                     i,j: INTEGER;
                     A: arrayof INTEGER;
                   end;
              end;
const initial_triple = triple(('0':m),0.0,(0,0,none ));
      m=200;

type T1 : array [1..3] of BOOLEAN:4;
const
   A1= T1(#X_A: 3);        -- A1 = (1010,1010,1010)
   A2= T1((#4_3:2): 3);    -- A2 = (1111,1111,1111)
                           -- #4_3:2 denotes here a boolean constant
```

6. Names and Expressions

6.1. Names

\<name\>::= \<simple name\> | \<indexed name\> | \<dotted name\> |
    \<binding name\>
References:
\<simple name\> --> 6.1.1, \<indexed name\> --> 6.1.2
\<dotted name\> --> 6.1.3, \<binding name\> --> 6.1.4

Names are formulae that allow to apply declared entities. The simplest form of a name is an applied occurrence of an identifier. More complicated are generators which serve for generating new objects and *adjustable arrays*. Particular forms of names are indexed names which serve for accessing *array components* and dotted names which serve for accessing *record components*, unit entities, type attributes and object attributes. Binding names allow to access entities which are hidden because of unit nesting.

6.1.1. Simple Names

\<simple name\>::= \<simple identifier\> | \<generator\>
\<simple identifier\>::= \<variable identifier\> | \<constant identifier\> |
    \<type identifier\> | \<unit identifier\> | \<signal identifier\>
\<generator\>::= \<class generator\> | \<array generator\> | \<copy operator\> |
    \<process generator\>
References:
\<variable identifier\> --> 5.1, \<constant identifier\> --> 5.2
\<type identifier\> --> 4, \<unit identifier\> --> 3.2,
\<signal identifier\> --> 17.1.1, \<class generator\> --> 4.5.1.2,
\<array generator\> --> 4.5.2.2, \<copy operator\> --> 4.5.3
\<process generator\> --> 16.1

The entity designated by a simple identifier is defined by binding rules (see 14). The value designated by a generator is the reference to the generated object (*adjustable array*).

6.1.2. Indexed Names

<indexed name>::= <name> [<expression list>]
<expression list>::= { <expression> ♯ , }+
References:
<name> --> 6.1, <expression> --> 6.2

An indexed name designates an *array component*. Hence, the name given in the indexed name must designate a *static array* or an *adjustable array* while the sequence of expressions must define the values of indices.

In the case of a *static array component* (see 4.3.1), the number of expressions must be equal to the number of indices and each expression must be of type consistent with the type of the corresponding index. If any index value is outside the range specified for the index, then a static-or-dynamic system signal Con_Error is raised (see 17.3). If the index type defines a specific signal for this situation, then this signal is raised instead of Con_Error. Otherwise an indexed name designates a *static array component* specified by the corresponding index values. No commitment is made to a particular order of index values computation.

For an *adjustable array component* (see 4.5.2.1) the following rule is applied. The type of an array A may be in the form of:

arrayof ... **arrayof** T

where **arrayof** is repeated n times and T is a type which is no longer in the form of **arrayof** S. An indexed name may be in the form of:

A[E1, E2 ,..., Ek]

where A is the name designating an *adjustable array*. Then the number of expressions k must be less or equal to the number of indices n, and each expression must be of any integer type. If a reference value designated by A is **none**, then the system signal Acc_Error is raised (see 17.3). Otherwise this value is the reference to an *adjustable array* A1 and an index value j1 specified by expression E1 is computed. If j1 is outside the index range of A1, the system signal Con_Error is raised (see 17.3). Otherwise the previous rule is applied to an *adjustable array* A2 designated by an indexed name A[E1]. And so on, the signal Acc_Error is raised, if an *adjustable array* Ai referred to by A[E1,...,Ei−1], 1<i<=k, is undefined and a signal error Con_Error is raised if the value ji of expression Ei is outside the index range of *adjustable array* Ai. Otherwise a value referred to by A[E1,...,Ei] is defined. The so-computed final result (for i=k) is a variable, which is an *adjustable array* component designated by an index name A[E1,...,Ek].

An indexed name may also designate the bit of a boolean value (see 4.1.3). Then the name given in the indexed name must be that of a boolean type and only one expression can appear in place of the sequence of expressions. This expression indicates the index of a corresponding bit. If the index value is outside of the length of the specified boolean type, then a static-or-dynamic system signal Con_Error is raised (see 17.3).

Examples:

    var A: **array** [1..10] **of** REAL;
       B: **array** [1..10] **of** array [1..10] **of** digit;
       B1: **array** [1..10,1..10] **of** digit;
       C: **array** [1..10] **of** arrayof INTEGER;
       C1: **arrayof** arrayof INTEGER;
       b: BOOLEAN:10; i,j: 1..10;

A[i]	−− a component of a one−dimensional static array A
B[i]	−− a component of a one−dimensional static array B
B[i][j]	−− a component of a component of a one−dimensional
	−− static array B
B1[i,j]	−− a component of a two−dimensional static array B1
C[i][j]	−− a component of an adjustable array C[i], where C is
	−− a one−dimensional static array with components of
	−− adjustable array types
C1[i,j]	−− a component of an adjustable array C1[i], where
	−− C1 is an adjustable array of adjustable arrays
b[i]	−− boolean variable designating the i−th bit of variable b

6.1.3. Dotted Names

<dotted name>::={ <expression> .{<simple identifier>|<component identifier> }}|
   {<name>.<simple identifier>}
References:
<expression> --> 6.2, <simple identifier> --> 6.1.1
<component identifier> --> 4.3.2, <name> --> 6.1

A dotted name of the form E.X, where E is an expression and X is a simple or component identifier, may designate a *record component* or an object attribute. It may also designate the predefined attribute of a *adjustable array* or of a string. If expression E is of a *record type*, identifier X must denote a component of this type value.

If expression E is of a *class type*, identifier X must denote an object attribute defined for this *class type* (see 4.5.1.1). Identifier X can also denote an *adjustable array attribute* (see 4.5.2.1), if expression E is of an *adjustable array type*. If the value of expression E is equal to **none**, then the system signal Acc_Error is raised (see 17.3).

A dotted name of the form N.X, where N is a *type name* and X is a simple identifier, designates a type attribute. In this case identifier X must denote an attribute of the type designated by name N.

Examples:

```
unit C: class;
    var b: BOOLEAN;
    const m=100;
    unit f: function (n:INTEGER): INTEGER;
    end f;
end C;
var X: OBJECT; Y: C; u: U; A: arrayof INTEGER;
type T : 1..100;
    U : record
            first: INTEGER;
            second: REAL;
        end;
C.m          -- an attribute of class C
C(X).b       -- an attribute b of object X
             -- qualified by class C (see 6.3)
Y.f(i)       -- a function call f(i), where f is an attribute
             -- of object Y
T.VAL(7)     -- predefined attribute of type T
u.first      -- a record component
A.LOWER      -- adjustable array attribute
```

6.1.4. Binding Names

<binding name>::={ <binding name> | <unit identifier> } ' <simple identifier>
References:
<unit identifier> −−> 3.2, <simple identifier> −−> 6.1.1

Binding names change binding rules for simple identifiers (see 14).

For a binding name of the form N'X N must be a unit name designating a unit enclosing this occurrence of N'X or a unit belonging to the inheritance sequence of such a unit. Thus the binding name N'X designates the local entity, identified by X, of the unit N associated according to the identfier binding rules (see 14.1).

Examples:

```
C: class;
    unit f: function (i:INTEGER): INTEGER;
        { this function will be referred to as fun1}
        unit init: class; var r: REAL; end;
        unit f: function (i: INTEGER): REAL;
            {this function will be referred to as fun2}
            unit sample: inherits init procedure (i: INTEGER);
                var r: REAL;
            begin
                i          −− parameter of sample
                f'i        −− parameter of fun2
                f(5)       −− call for real function fun2
                C'f(5)     −− call for integer function fun1
                r          −− local variable declared in procedure sample
                init'r     −− local variable declared in class init
            end sample; . . .
        end f; . . .
    end f; . . .
end C;
```

6.2. Expressions

The syntax of the expressions given below does not distinguish all the possible forms of arithmetic and boolean subexpressions. They will be described by semantic rules presented in the corresponding subsections.

<expression>::=
    {{{<negation>}?{<sign>}?{<simple expression> ∦ <arithmetic operator>}+}
    ∦ <boolean operator>}+
<simple expression>::= <literal> | <name> | <function call> |
    (<expression>) | <qualified expression>
<literal>::= <numeric literal> | <boolean literal> |
    <character literal> | <string literal> | <enumeration literal> |
    <reference literal>

References:
<sign> --> 2.5, <arithmetic operator> --> 6.2.2
<negation> --> 6.2.3, <boolean operator> --> 6.2.3
<numeric literal> --> 2.5, <boolean literal> --> 2.6
<character literal> --> 2.7, <string literal> --> 2.8
<enumeration literal> --> 4.2.1, <reference literal> --> 4.5
<name> --> 6.1, <function call> --> 10.2
<qualified expression> --> 6.3

A literal denotes an explicit value of a given type (see 4.1.1, 4.1.2, 4.1.3, 4.1.4, 4.1.5, 4.2.1). The reference literal **none** (see 4.5) denotes the undefined reference value of any reference type.

6.2.1. Expression Computation

Names are computed in order defined by the syntax. The computation order of arithmetic and boolean expressions is induced by the precedence of operators given in the following table (in increasing order from 1 to 9):

operator	syntax	references
1 disjunctions	**or, xor**	6.2.3
2 conjunction	**and**	6.2.3
3 concatenation	**&**	6.2.3
4 negation	**not**	6.2.3
5 relational operators	$=,=/=,<,<=,>,>=$	6.2.3
	is, in	12.2
6 adding operators	$+,-$	6.2.2
7 sign	$+,-$	6.2.2
8 multiplying operators	$*,/,$**mod**	6.2.2
9 exponentiating operator	$**$	6.2.2

For any expression operators of higher precedence are applied first. If a sequence of operators is of the same precedence, then they are applied in textual order from left to right. Parentheses can be used to impose another order of expression computation, i.e. the expressions in parentheses are to be computed first. For all other situations the language does not force any special order of operator application. For instance, the order of computation of two operands of any binary operator is not defined.

Examples:

k∗j∗∗10	−− j∗∗10 is computed first
−x/2.0+3.5	−− x/2.0 is computed first, then −x/2.0
z+REAL(k−j)	−− (k−j) is computed first, then REAL is applied
i **mod** j+k	−− i **mod** j is computed first
(a+b)∗(c+d)	−− c+d may be computed before a+b
T(X).b	−− T(X) is computed first
x<y **and** R1=R2 **or** i=j	−− x<y, R1=R2, i=j may be computed in any order,
	−− but **and** must be computed before **or**
x < y < b	−− x < y is computed first, so if b is of
	−− type BOOLEAN, then the expression is correct
x/y/z	−− x/y is computed first, then
	−− the result is divided by z
d∗C(B).f(x,y).e	−− C(B)is computed first, then successively
	−− dotted name C(B).f
	−− function call C(B).f(x,y),
	−− dotted name C(B).f(x,y).e,
	−− which is finally multiplied by d

6.2.2. Arithmetic Expressions

Arithmetic expressions are formulae which define the computation of numeric values.

<arithmetic operator>::= <exponentiating operator> |
   <multiplying operator> | <adding operator>
<exponentiating operator>::= **
<multiplying operator>::= * | / | **mod**
<adding operator>::= + | −

Sign + (as unary operator) denotes identity, sign − (as unary operator) denotes arithmetic negation. In both cases the result is of the type of the operand. The predefined function ABS (see 4.1.1 and 4.1.2) denotes the absolute value and returns the result of the type of the argument.

For binary operators $+, -, *, /,$ **mod** the admissible categories of types for operands and for the result are given in the following table (where "integer" denotes any integer type and "real" denotes any real type):

operator	left operand	right operand	result
$+,-,*,/$	integer	integer	integer
	real	real	real
mod	integer	integer	integer
**	integer	integer	integer
	real	integer	real

The type of the result is defined by the types of the arguments. For arguments of types INTEGER : n1 and INTEGER : n2 the type of the result is INTEGER : max(n1,n2).

For arguments of types REAL : m1 : e1 and REAL : m2 : e2 the type of the result is REAL : max(m1,m2) : max(e1,e2). For exponentiation the result is of the type of the left argument.

An arithmetic operation on two integer subtypes (see 4.2.2) will produce the result of type which is the minimal subtype interval containing both operand subtypes.

Operator + (as binary operator) denotes addition, operator − (as binary operator) denotes subtraction, operator ∗ denotes multiplication and operator / denotes division. Division of integer values i=n/m and modulus j=n **mod** m are determined by the equation:

$$n = m*i + j$$

where ABS(j) < ABS(m) and j<0 iff m<0.

Exponentiating by a positive exponent is equivalent to repeated multiplication of the left operand by itself. Exponentiating to 0 gives 1 or 1.0, respectively to the type of the left operand. If for a real type the exponent is negative, the result is the reciprocal of the value with the positive exponent. For an integer type of the left operand the negative exponent gives the result which is the integer reciprocal of the value with the positive exponent, e.g. (−2)∗∗(−1)=−1, 1∗∗(−1)=1, 2∗∗(−1)=0.

An arithmetic operation may raise the system signal Num_Error (see 17.3) if the result does not lie within the range of the implemented numeric type. Typically Num_Error is raised when a division by zero appears, however in many other situations (e.g. overflow, underflow) this signal may also be raised.

Examples:

```
k*j**10          -- integer, if k and j are integer
-x/2.0+3.5       -- real, if x is real
z+REAL(k-j)      -- real, if z is real
i mod j+k        -- integer
```

6.2.3. Boolean Expressions

Boolean expressions are formulae which define the computations of boolean values.

<negation>::= **not**

<boolean operator>::= <relational operator> | <logical operator>

<relational operator>::= <equality operator> | <order operator> |
    <membership operator>

<equality operator>::= = | =/=

<order operator>::= < | <= | > | >=

<logical operator>::= & | **and** | **or** | **xor**

References:

<membership operator> --> 12.2

For the equality relation E1=E2 (E1=/=E2) the expressions E1 and E2 must be of consistent (see 4.6) numeric, boolean, discrete, or reference types. The result is of type BOOLEAN, and has the value according to the test on equality (see 4.1.1., 4.1.2., 4.1.3., 4.1.4, 4.2, 4.5).

For order relations E1<E2, E1<=E2, E1>E2, E1>=E2, both expressions E1 and E2 must be of consistent numeric, boolean or discrete types. The result is of type BOOLEAN, and gives the value according to the test for ordering (see 4.1.1., 4.1.2, 4.1.3, 4.1.4, 4.2).

For membership relations consult 12.2.

Boolean operators **not** (logical negation), **and** (conjunction), **or** (inclusive disjunction) and **xor** (exclusive disjunction) are applied for single boolean values as well as for sequences of boolean values (see 4.1.3). Operator **not** gives the result of the same type as of the given operand. Operators **and, or** and **xor** must have both operands of the same boolean type. The result is of the operands type. All these operations are performed simultaneously on all the positions of the corresponding operands.

Operation E1&E2 defines concatenation of boolean sequences specified by the expressions E1 and E2 (it defines also a concatenation of string constants, see 4.1.5, 6.2.4). The expressions E1 and E2 may be of any boolean types, i.e. if E1 is of type BOOLEAN:c1 and E2 is of type BOOLEAN:c2, then the result is of type BOOLEAN:c1+c2.

Examples:

        x<y **and** R1=R2 **or** i=j   -- the result is of type BOOLEAN
        b1 & b2   -- if b1 is of type BOOLEAN:10
                                 -- and b2 is of type BOOLEAN:5, then
                                 -- the result is of type BOOLEAN:15

6.2.4. Static Expressions

Static expressions specify values computable at compilation time. Hence, every static expression must be of one of the following forms:

(1) a literal,

(2) a constant,

(3) a predefined type attribute T.FIRST, T.LAST, T.SIZE, T.SIZE_M or T.SIZE_E,

(4) a predefined type attribute PRED, SUCC, POS or T.VAL applied to an argument defined by a static expression,

(5) a dotted name defining a component of a record constant,

(6) an indexed name defining a component of a *static array constant*, or a component of a boolean constant, where the expressions defining indices are static expressions,

(7) a qualified static expression,

(8) an arithmetic or a boolean expression with all its constituents being static expressions,

(9) a concatenation of static expressions designating strings or characters.

Examples:

```
B[2]+7              -- where B is a constant array
INTEGER(pi-0.7)     -- where pi is a constant real value
#X_00A0:2 & 1<i*j   -- where i and j are constant integers
C.A[7]              -- where C is a constant record with
                    -- a component A which is a static array
PRED(day.LAST)      -- where day is an enumeration type
"A simple ter"&'m'  -- the concatenation of a string with a character
                    -- gives a string constant
```

6.3. Qualifications

<qualified expression>::= <type name> (<expression>)
References:
<type name> --> 4, <expression> --> 6.2

A qualification is used to state or to change the type of an expression (see 6.2). The change of an expression type may involve also the change of a value representation (conversion).

Expression E of type S may be qualified by a type identifier T consistent with S (see 4.7). Only expressions of numeric types, discrete types, subtypes and class types can be qualified. The result of qualification is the expression of type T. The value of the qualified expression must belong to the set determined by type T.

For numeric types in the situations listed below the above condition is checked after conversion.

(1) Qualification of a real type by another real type with less accuracy forces rounding-off of the qualified value to this accuracy.

(2) Qualification of a real type by an integer type forces truncation of the real value.

(3) Qualification of an integer type by a real type forces conversion of the integer value to the isomorphic real value which is later rounded off to the required accuracy.

If the qualified value is not of type T, then a static-or-dynamic signal Con_Error is raised (see 17.3), unless the type T raises a special signal for exceeding its range.

For *class types*, only a qualification within a dotted name is possible. In a dotted name T(E).X, expression E of *class type* S may be qualified by an identifier T denoting a *class type* consistent with S (see 4.7). If the value of expression E is not of type T, then the system signal Acc_Error is raised (see 17.3). Otherwise the type of the expression T(E) is changed to T.

Examples:

```
long_integer(100_000_000)    -- long constant
REAL(i*j)                    -- conversion to REAL
working_day(PRED(Q))         -- expression qualified by a subtype
C(X).a                       -- attribute a of the object
                             -- denoted by X, qualified by C
```

7. Statements

Statements are patterns for executing some actions.

<executive part>::=

   begin <sequence of statements> {<lastwill statements>}?

<sequence of statements>::= { <statement> # ; }⁺

<statement>::= <simple statement> | <compound statement>

References:

<simple statement> --> 7.1, <compound statement> --> 7.2

<lastwill statements> --> 17.1.4

A simple statement contains no other statements while a compound statement may contain simple statements and other compound statements.

7.1. Simple Statements

<simple statement>::= <control statement> | <configuration statement> |

   <assignment statement> | <empty statement> | <i/o statement>

<control statement>::= <loop control statement> | <return statement> |

   <inner statement> | <coroutine control statement> |

   <communication statement> | <exception control statement>

<configuration statement>::= <procedure call> | <kill statement> |

   <block> | <raise statement> | <new statement> |

   <alien call> | <send statement>

<assignment statement>::= <name> := <expression>

<empty statement>::=

<return statement>::= **return** | <return from alien call >

<new statement>::= <class generator>

References:

<loop control statement> --> 7.2.3, <inner statement> --> 12.4

<coroutine control statement> --> 15.2, <communication statement> --> 16.2

<exception control statement> --> 17.1.4

<procedure call> --> 10.2, <kill statement> --> 4.5.4

<block> --> 13, <raise statement> --> 17.1.3

<alien call> --> 16.2, <send statement> --> 16.3,

<return from alien call> --> 16.2,

<name> --> 6.1, <expression> --> 6.2

<i/o statement> --> 18.3, <class generator> --> 4.5.1.2

In an assignment statement in the form of:

N:=E

the type of name N must be of type consistent (see 4.7) with the type of expression E.

In the case of subprogram assignments, expression E as well as name N must be a subprogram name. In such a case the condition that the type of E should replace the type of N is checked (see 4.6, 4.7).

In the case of integer to real or real to integer assignments, expression E is implicitly qualified (see 6.3) to the type of variable N. For the execution of an assignment statement the variable designated by name N is first computed. Then the value of expression E is computed. This value must belong to the set determined by the type of variable N. If not, then the static-or-dynamic system signal Con_Error is raised (see 17.3), unless the type of variable defines a special signal for exceeding its range. Finally the value of expression E is assigned to the variable designated by name N. This rule concerns simple values as well as composite values, when all the components of the composite value are assigned.

It may happen that the computation of name N or expression E will cause the deallocation of an instance where the designated variable is situated. Then the system signal Acc_Error is raised (see 17.3) at the execution of an assignment statement.

The execution of an empty statement has no other effect than to pass to the next action. The execution of a *return statement* causes the termination of a unit instance (see 10.2, 12.4, 15.1, 16.1, 17.1.4). The execution of a *new statement* has the same effect as the execution of a *class generator* (see 4.5.1.2), however the reference given as the value of the generator is not used.

Examples:

x:=i	-- if x is of real type and i is of integer type,
	-- then the implicit type conversion from integer
	-- to real type is performed
i:=x	-- type conversion from real to integer type
B[i][j+k]:=k−1	-- first the variable B[i][j+k] is computed,
	-- then the value of expression k−1 is computed
	-- and it is assigned to the computed variable
z:=z1	-- if z and z1 are record variables of the same
	-- type, then all components of z1 will be
	-- assigned to the corresponding components of z
z:=z1	-- if z and z1 are static array variables of the
	-- same type, then all the components of z1 will be
	-- assigned to the corresponding components of z
z:=z1	-- if z and z1 are reference variables, then
	-- the reference value of z1 is assigned to z

7.2. Compound Statements

<compound statement>::= <conditional statement> | <case statement> |
   <loop statement>
References:
<conditional statement> --> 7.2.1, <case statement> --> 7.2.2
<loop statement> --> 7.2.3

7.2.1. Conditional Statements

<conditional statement>::=
   if <condition>
   then <sequence of statements>
   {<else part>}?
   fi
<condition>::= <expression> { { <orif list> }? | { <andif list> }? }
<orif list>::= { **orif** <expression> }+
<andif list>::= { **andif** <expression> }+
<else part>::= **else** <sequence of statements>
References:
<expression> --> 6.2, <sequence of statements> --> 7

In a conditional statement in the form of:
   if B
   then
      G1
   else
      G2
   fi

B must be a boolean expression of type BOOLEAN (see 6.2.3) and G1, G2 must be sequences of statements. For the value of B equal TRUE sequence G1 is executed. Otherwise
sequence G2 is executed.

In a conditional statement in the form of:
   if B1 **orif** B2 ... **orif** Bj
   then
      G1
   else
      G2
   fi

the boolean expressions B1,...,Bj (of type BOOLEAN) are computed in succession until the first one from the left Bi, $1<=i<=j$, evaluates to TRUE. Then sequence G1 of statements is executed. If none of the conditions B1,...,Bj are satisfied, then sequence G2 is executed.

If an *andif list* occurs instead of an *orif list*, then the expressions B1,...,Bj are computed in succession until the first one from the left Bi, $1<=i<=j$, evaluates to FALSE; then sequence G2 is executed. If all the conditions B1, ...,Bj are satisfied, then sequence G1 is executed.

The conditional statement with the *else part* omitted is equivalent to the conditional statement with the empty *else part*.

Examples:

```
if delta > 0
then
      x2:=sqrt(delta)/a/2;
      if b = 0
      then
            x1:=−x2
      else
            x1:=−b/a/2+x2; x2:=x1−2∗x2
      fi
else
      if delta = 0
      then
            x1:=−b/a/2; x2:=x1;
      else
            write ("no real roots")
      fi
fi

if i > n orif A[i]=0
then
      i:=i−1
else
      A[i]:=1
fi
```

7.2.2. Case Statements

<case statement>::=
    case <expression>
      { <when part> }$^+$
      {<else part>}?
    esac
<when part>::=
    when { {<expression> | <bound pair>} ⫴ ,}$^+$:
    <sequence of statements>
References:
<expression> ‒‒> 6.2, <sequence of statements> ‒‒> 7
<bound pair> ‒‒> 4.2.2, <else part> ‒‒> 7.2.1.

All expressions appearing in a *case statement* must be of a discrete, character or integer type. Expressions in *when parts* must be static and their values must belong to the type of the expression appearing after **case**. Each when part defines a list of expressions and bound pairs. Each expression in the list defines a constant. Each bound pair in the list defines a finite set of constants belonging to the specified interval. In this way each when part defines a finite set of constants. All thus defined finite sets must be pairwise disjoint. For execution of the following *case statement*:

    case E
      when E1 : G1
       ...
      when Ek : Gk
      else G
    esac

where G1,...,Gk,G denote sequences of statements and E1,...,Ek denote expression lists and/or bound pairs, first the value of expression E is computed. Then a sequence Gi, $1<=i<=k$, where the value of E belongs to the sequence of constants specified by Ei, is selected for execution. The choice of *else part* covers all values (possibly none) not given in the previous choices, and then sequence G is executed.

If the value of expression E does not belong to any specified set, then the system signal Con_Error is raised.

Examples:

```
case n+1
    when 1,12..17,20: n:=n+1; x:=0.1
    when −1,3,55:    n:=n−1; x:=−0.1
    else write ("wrong data")
esac
case current_day
    when Mon..Fri: writeln ("go to work")
    when Sat,Sun:  writeln ("weekend")
esac
case n
    when 0..9 :    write ("digit")
    when 10..15 :   write ("hexadecimal digit")
    else write ("not digit")
esac
```

7.2.3. Loop Statements

\<loop statement\>::= \<do statement\> | \<while statement\> | \<for statement\>
\<do statement\>::=
  do
   \<sequence of statements\>
  od
\<loop control statement\>::= {**exit** }$^+$ { **repeat** }?
\<while statement\>::= **while** \<condition\> \<do statement\>
\<for statement\>::= **for** \<control variable identifier\> \<range\>
  \<do statement\>
\<range\>::= {:= \<range bounds\> | **in** \<type name\> }
\<range bounds\>::= \<expression\> {\<step part\>}? { **to** | **downto** } \<expression\>
\<step part\>::= **step** \<expression\>
\<control variable identifier\>::= \<identifier\>
References:
\<sequence of statements\> --> 7
\<condition\> --> 7.2.1, \<identifier\> --> 2.2
\<type name\> --> 4, \<expression\> --> 6.2

The following *do statement*:
```
do
 G
od
```

causes the iteration of the sequence of statements G. The execution of the loop may be abandoned as the result of a loop control statement *exit* executed in G. In general, the loop control statement makes it possible to leave a number of nested loops, or to skip the remaining statements in the loop and to start the next iterations.

The loop control statement H of the form **exit...exit** (k−times) where k>=1 may occur in j (j>=0) nested *do statements* Gj, ..., G1, i.e. statement Gj−1 is nested in Gj, Gj−2 in Gj−1, etc. and finally, statement H appears in G1, but not in any nested *do statement* inside G1. Let M be the smallest unit enclosing these statements Gj,...,G1. Then:

(1) If k=j+1, then the execution of H causes the termination of the unit body M (jump to the final *end symbol*).

(2) If k<=j, then the execution of statement H causes the termination of *do statement* Gk.

(3) If k>j+1, then statement H is syntactically incorrect.

The keyword **repeat** may occur just after the sequence of *exit*'s in the loop control statement H. If k<j, then *do statement* Gk terminates and the iteration of *do statement* is continued without the execution of the statements occurring after statement Gk in *do statement* Gk+1. If k>=j, then such a loop control statement is syntactically incorrect.

The following diagram illustrates some of the above described situations:

```
      begin                      —— begin of M
        ...
        do                       —— begin of Gk+1
 {1}    ...                      —— first statement in Gk+1
          do                     —— begin of Gk
          ...
            do                   —— begin of G1
              exit...exit        —— when k=j+1 skip to 3
              exit...exit        —— when k<=j continue from 2
              exit...exit repeat —— when k<j continue from 1
            od ;                 —— end of G1
            ...
          od ;                   —— end of Gk
 {2}    ...                      —— first statement after Gk
        od ;                     —— end of Gk+1
        ...
 {3}  end ;                      —— end of M
```

A *while statement* of the form:
>**while B**
>**do**
> **G**
>**od**

is equivalent to the following *do statement*:

>**do if B then G else exit fi od**

where B denotes any condition, i.e. a single boolean expression, an *orif list* or an *andif list*.

For statements are of the following three forms:
(*) **for i:=E1 step E2 to E3 do G od**
(**) **for i:=E1 step E2 downto E3 do G od**
(***) **for i in T do G od**

where the *step part* in (*) and (**) is optional. All three expressions E1, E2, E3 must be of the type consistent with an integer or a character or an enumeration type. *Type name* T (see 6.1) must designate a discrete or character type. The *step part* must be omitted in the case of a non-integer type (and then its value corresponds to the positioning of the given type), and may be omitted if the value of E2 equals 1 in the case of an integer type.

Control variable i is implicitly declared and is of an integer, a discrete, or a character type consistent with the types of expressions E1, E2, E3, in cases (*) and (**), or with T, in case (***). Its accessibility scope is the corresponding loop, i.e. the sequence of statements G. Variable i must not appear on the left hand side of an assignment statement neither as an actual parameter standing for an *output* or *inout formal parameter* in sequence G.

All three kinds of *for statements* cause the iteration of the sequence of statements G for the values of control variable i changing according to the specified range. In case (*) the value of variable i starts from the value of E1 and after each iterative step is increased by the value of E2. If the value of variable i becomes greater than the value of E3, then the execution of this *for statement* ends. In case (**) the value of variable i starts from the value of E1 and after each iterative step is decreased by the value of E2. If the value of variable i becomes less than the value of E3, then the execution of this *for statement* ends. Statement (***) is equivalent to the following statement:

for i:=T.FIRST to T.LAST do G od

where the default value of the step corresponds to the positioning of type T.

In all these three cases the values determining the specified range (e.g. the values of expressions E1, E2 and E3) are computed once, before the execution of such a *for statement* begins.

A loop control statement (i.e. *exit* or *repeat statement*) may appear not only in a normal *do statement* but also in a *while statement* or in a *for statement*. If a single *exit statement* is executed in a *while statement* or in a *for statement*, then it ends the execution of such a loop statement. If a single *repeat statement* is executed in a *while statement*, then the next iteration continues from the verification of the condition. If a single *repeat statement* is executed in a *for statement*, then the next iteration continues from the computation of a new value of the control variable.

Examples:

```
{ Sequential search, e.g. search for x=A[j] in A: array [1..n] of REAL }
found:=FALSE;
for j:=1 to n
do
    if x=A[j] then found:=TRUE; exit fi;
od;
{ Pattern matching, e.g. search for all occurrences of
    pattern: array [1..m] of CHAR in
    text: array [1..n] of CHAR }
for i:=1 to n−m+1
do
    k:=i;
    for j:=1 to m
    do
        if pattern[j] =/= text[k] then exit repeat fi;
        k:=k+1
    od;
    write (i)
od;
{ Inorder traversal of a binary tree with the help of a stack.Search for a node p
    such that p.element=x. Tree begins withthe node root and each node p has two
    sons, p.left and p.right }
p:=root; top:=0;
do
    while p.left =/= none
    do
        top:=top+1; stack[top]:=p; p:=p.left
    od;
    do  if p.element=x then found:=TRUE; exit exit fi;
        if p.right=/=none then p:=p.right; exit fi;
        if top=0 then found:=FALSE; exit exit fi;
        p:=stack[top]; top:=top−1
    od
od;
```

8. Unit Specification, Unit Body and Entities Accessibility

8.1. Complete Unit Definition

<complete unit>::= <unit specification> <unit body>
<unit specification>::= **unit** <unit identifier>: <unit head> ; <declarative part>
<unit head>::= <subprogram head> | <class head> |
    <coroutine head> | <process head>
<unit body>::= { <body head> }? <declarative part>
    <executive part> <end part>
<body head>::= **body** {;}?
<end part>::= **end** {<unit identifier>}?
References:
<subprogram head> --> 10.1, <class head> --> 11,
<coroutine head> --> 15.1, <process head> --> 16.1,
<declarative part> --> 3.3, <executive part> --> 7
<unit identifier> --> 3.2

A declarative part in a unit specification may be non-empty only for classes. The optional body head may appear only for classes, if the following declarative part is nonempty. If an optional identifier appears in the *end part*, it must match a unit identifier.

A unit specification serves as an interface to the other units. Every entity declared within a unit specification may be accessed from outside of the textual range of the unit declaration.

A unit body is a private part of the unit. It allows to encapsulate the implementation details of a unit. The textual range of a unit body constitutes a barrier for accessibility of entities which are declared within this range. From outside this range their declarations are treated as nonexistent and thus none of them can be accessed from there. Consequently, the accessibility scope of an entity is the textual range of the unit body most tightly enclosing the defining occurrence of this entity. Such an accessibility restriction permits the user to protect selected entities against unauthorized access. It also assures that the compilation of any unit from outside of a given unit body textual range is completely independent from the unit body contents.

For subprograms only parameters may be accessed from outside by means of parameter transmission. Therefore a subprogram head alone forms a subprogram specification and the remaining part of its declaration is considered to be a subprogram body.

the declarative part of a class may be split into two different declarative parts by the keyword **body**. The first part is a *class specification* while the second part is a *class body*.

The entities declared in a specification part of a class may be freely accessed from outside of this class by means of dotted names or due to inheritance, while the entities declared within a *class body* are accessible only in its textual range. As both declarative parts contain declarations of local entities they must obey the general rule of uniqueness of identifier association within a unit (see 3.3).

If a class does not contain the keyword **body** its declaration part belongs to the specification part and its body starts with the executive part.

Examples:

```
unit A: class;
  var x1: INTEGER;
  unit f1: function : INTEGER;
    begin RESULT:=x1 end;
body;
  var x2: INTEGER;
  unit f2: function : INTEGER;
    begin RESULT:=x2 end;
begin . . .
end A;
```

Variable x1 and function f1 may be accessed from outside of A e.g. by dotted names (see 6.1.3). Variable x2 and function f2 may be accessed only within the range between *body* and *end* of A. This example actually offers nothing more than can be obtained by applying a *block statement*. A description of the full power of unit specification and unit body is provided in the next section.

8.2. Separate Specification and Continued Unit Declaration

\<separate specification\>::= **unit** \<unit identifier\>: \<unit head\>
  { ; \<declarative part\> \<end part\>}? \<continuation sign\>
\<continued unit declaration\>::= \<continuation sign\>
  { **unit** \<unit identifier\>: \<unit body\>
  | \<complete unit\> }
\<continuation sign\>::= −\>
References:
\<unit identifier\> −−\> 3.2, \<unit head\> −−\> 8.1
\<declarative part\> −−\> 3.3, \<end part\> −−\> 8.1
\<unit body\> −−\> 8.1, \<complete unit\> −−\> 8.1

In a separate specification a declarative part and an *end part* may appear only for classes. When a unit body is used in the production rule for continued unit declaration, then the optional body head (see 8.1) must be present.

Unit specification and unit body need not be provided in one textually contiguous part. If a unit is declared within a class, then its declaration may be split into two parts. The unit specification (for classes even part of it) may be separated from the continued unit declaration which is the rest of the unit. Continuation sign virtually replaces the remaining part of the declaration for each of the separated parts.

A separate specification declared within the specification of a unit should be continued within the body of this unit. A separate specification declared within the separate specification of another unit should be continued within the continued unit declaration of that unit. A separate specification should not be declared within a unit body. A separate specification and a continued declaration of the same unit must be declared with the same unit identifier.

Examples:

```
unit C: class;
    var x1: REAL;
    unit f: function (x: REAL):REAL −>;   −− separate specification of f
    unit f1: function (x: REAL):REAL;
      begin RESULT := x + x1
    end f1;
```

```
body
    var x2: REAL;
    ->unit f: body                        -- body of f
        begin RESULT := x + x2            -- in form of
    end f;                                -- continued declaration
    unit f2: function (x: REAL):REAL;
        begin RESULT := x + x2
    end f2;
    begin
    x2 := ...
end C;
```

The main motivation for separating a unit specification is to extend accessibility scope of the declared unit. Function f can be called from outside of class C, but f2 cannot.

Variable x2 is protected against unauthorized access from outside of class C body. However x2 may be used from there via f. Function f controls in this sense the access to x2. Function f1 has no opportunity of this as it sees no declaration of x2 in class C.

The continued declaration in the form of a unit body is nothing more than the textual separation of a unit body from a unit specification.

The continued declaration in the form of a complete unit gives the opportunity of repeating the unit head. The repeated head must satisfy the following conditions:

(1) the original and the repeated head must specify the same unit kind,

(2) both heads should inherit the same class, if any,

(3) both heads should specify semantically equivalent parameter list (see 9.2),

(4) in the case of functions the result types specified by both heads should be semantically equivalent (see 4.7).

Two declarative parts are admitted only for classes (see 8.1). The first one may appear in the specification part of a unit, while the latter one may appear in the body of this unit. This latter one has the same meaning as for ordinary *class body* declaration, but the first one is not merely the repetition of the declaration part from the separate specification. It may introduce new local entities for such a *class declaration* (but the uniqueness of identifier association within a unit must be preserved).

The accessibility scope of the entities declared in the first declarative part is wider than in the unit body because they are declared outside of it. On the other hand their accessibility is still more restricted than the accessibility of the entities declared in the separate specification, since the separate specification lies outside of the unit body most closely enclosing the continued declaration. Such an accessibility nuances are sometimes substantial for designing proper entities protection, as on the following example.

Examples:

```
unit Push_down : class;                   —— Push_down store for integer numbers
    unit elem: class;                     —— separate specification of elem
        var i: INTEGER;                   —— i is visible for any Push_down user
    end elem −>;                          —— as integer located onto the stack
    unit pop: function : elem −>;
    unit push: procedure (x:elem) −>;
body;                                     —— implements store as a list structure
    var top: elem;

    { continued declaration of elem is in form of complete unit }
    −>unit elem: class;    —— this is the repeated head
        var next: elem;      —— next is visible within Push_down body
    end elem;
    −> unit pop:body;
      begin
        RESULT:= top; top:=top.next;
    end pop;
    −> unit push: body;
      begin
        x.next:= top; top:= x
    end push;
end Push_down;
```

The value of variable *next* is a reference to the next list element. It is not visible to a *Push_down* user, although it is substantial for a Push_down implementation. Variable *next* is not declared in the unit body of *elem* (but it is declared in a continued unit declaration of *elem*), so it is visible within the whole *Push_down* body. This restricted accessibility scope of *next* is necessary for proper implementation of function *pop* and procedure *push*.

9. Unit Parameterization

<formal parameter list>::= {
  ({ {<input parameters declaration> | <output parameters declaration> |
  <inout parameters declaration> } ⫲ ; }+) }?
<actual parameter list>::= { (<expression list>) }?
References:
<input parameters declaration> --> 9.1, <output parameters declaration> --> 9.1
<inout parameters declaration> --> 9.1, <expression list> --> 6.1.2

A unit may be parameterized by associating a formal parameter list. Each formal parameter of a unit is its local entity. The applied occurrences of identifiers within formal parameter list are bound as if they occur outside of the parameterized unit (see 14). For every unit without inheritance part (except blocks), its formal parameter list is fully specified in the unit head. For a unit inheriting a class (see 12), the formal parameter list is the concatenation of the formal parameter list of the inherited class and the list specified in the unit head.

If a unit is parameterized, an actual parameter list must be associated with its formal parameter list for each instance of this unit. Both lists must be of the same length. A positional correspondence between formal and actual parameters is established, i.e. each actual parameter corresponds to the formal parameter which stands at the same position in the formal parameter list.

An actual parameter list is given at the place of a unit instance generation, i.e. in a *class generator* (4.5.1.2), a *block statement* with inheritance part (13) or a subprogram call (10.2). Each actual parameter is an expression or a subprogram name.

Before the parameterized unit instance is generated, its actual parameters are computed. The language does not define an order in which the actual parameters of a unit instance are computed.

When the unit instance is generated, the initial transmission of actual to formal parameters is performed. When the unit instance execution is terminated, the final transmission of formal parameters to the corresponding actual parameters takes place.

9.1. Parameter Passing Modes

<input parameters declaration>::= {**input** }? <specification list>
<output parameters declaration>::= **output** <specification list>
<inout parameters declaration>::= **inout** <specification list>
References:
<specification list> −−> 5.1

Parameters of *input mode* are passed during initial transmission. If mode specification is omitted, then parameters are treated by default as *input* until an explicit mode specification is encountered in a parameter list. An actual parameter corresponding to the formal *input one* must be an expression or a subprogram name. First the value of an actual parameter is computed. Next, the value of the actual parameter is assigned to the corresponding formal variable (see 7.1). The reaction on detected errors is the same as in the case of assignment statement.

Parameters of *output mode* are passed during final transmission. An actual parameter corresponding to the formal one must be a variable name. A variable designated by an actual parameter is computed at the unit instance generation. When the unit instance execution is terminated the final value of the formal parameter is assigned to this variable (see 7.1). The reaction on detected errors is the same as in the case of assignment statement.

Parameters of *inout mode* represent the combined method. An actual parameter corresponding to the formal one must be a variable name. When the unit instance is generated, both a variable designated by the actual parameter and its value are computed. Then the computed value is assigned to the corresponding formal variable. When the instance execution is terminated, the final value of the formal parameter is assigned to the variable designated by the actual parameter. The reaction on errors is as in the other cases.

Examples:

```
unit elem: class (i: INTEGER; next: elem); { both parameters are input }
end elem;


unit swap: procedure (inout x,y: OBJECT);
var z: OBJECT;
begin
  z := x; x := y; y := z
end swap;
```

---

var e1,e2: elem;
swap(e1, e2)   –– exchange of the reference values of e1 and e2
swap(e1, e1.next)   –– the correct exchange of the reference values of
                      –– e1 and e1.next, since both variables e1, e1.next
                      –– are computed upon an entry to procedure swap,
                      –– i.e. no side effect like in the sequence:
                      –– z := e1; e1 := e1.next; e1.next := z

unit bisec: **function** (f:**function** (x:REAL): REAL; a,b,eps: REAL) : REAL;

type G: **procedure** (j:INTEGER;p:G);

unit r:G;
begin
  p(10,r);
end r;

9.2. Parameter List Consistency

Parameter list consistency concerns two notions: parameter list replacement and parameter list semantic equivalence. The first notion comes into play for subprogram types (see 4.6) and for virtual subprograms (see 12.5). The latter one is used for parameter list consistency of signal handlers (see 17.1.2) and continued unit declarations (see 8.2).

A formal parameter list is may be replaced by another formal parameter list iff the following conditions hold:

(1) both parameter lists are of the same length, however the corresponding parameters may be specified by different identifiers (in the case of inheritance the length of parameter list is defined in 12.3),

(2) the corresponding formal parameters are of the same passing modes,

(3) the type of a parameter from the first list may be replaced by the type of the corresponding parameter from the latter one (see 4.7).

Examples:

    type G: **function** (r:REAL):REAL;

    A: **class** (x:REAL;g:**function** (x:REAL;**output** z:REAL;b:B; f1:G):B);

    F: **function** (y:REAL;**output** t:REAL;**output** b:B1;f:G):B2;

    F1: **function** (x,y:REAL;**output** b:B; f:G):B;

    new A(15.0,F); $--$ correct iff B may be replaced by B1 and by B2
    new A(15.0,F1); $--$ incorrect since the second parameter
                                  $--$ of F1 is not of output mode

For continued unit declarations (8.2) and signal handlers (see 17.1.2) the notion of semantic equivalence of parameter lists is used. One list is semantically equivalent to another one iff the above three conditions hold with the notion of type replacement substituted by the notion of semantic type equivalence.

Examples:

    Main_block: **block**
    type T: **array** [1..10] **of** INTEGER;
    unit P: **procedure** (par:T); . . . **end** P;
    unit C: **class**;
        type T: **record**
                first: INTEGER;
                second: REAL;
            end;
        unit P1: **procedure** (x: Main_block'T); . . . **end** P1;
        unit P2: **procedure** (par:T); . . . **end** P2;
        . . .
    end C;
    . . .
    end Main_block

{ Parameter list of P1 is semantically equivalent to that of P. }

{ Parameter list of P2 is not semantically equivalent to that of P, because type T from class C is not semantically equivalent to type T from Main_block. }

10. Subprograms

There are two kinds of subprograms: *procedures* and *functions*. *Procedures* may be called only by a special statement (call statement, see 10.2) while *functions* return some values, and consequently, may be called only in expressions (see 6.2). A subprogram may inherit a *class* (see 12).

10.1. Subprogram Declaration

<subprogram head>::= <function head> | <procedure head> | <type name>
<function head>::= {<inheritance part>}? <function type>
<procedure head>::= {<inheritance part>}? <procedure type>
References:
<type name> --> 4, <function type> --> 4.6
<procedure type> --> 4.6, <inheritance part> --> 12

A subprogram head may be defined by a *type name* (a *subprogram type*) or by an explicit head. If a subprogram head is specified by a *type name*, then its meaning is defined by this *type declaration*.

In each function the predefined variable RESULT of the type specified in the function specification is implicitly declared. The value returned by the function is defined by the most recent value of this variable.

If a subprogram declaration appears in a specification part of a *class declaration*, then this subprogram is a virtual one. If such a virtual subprogram is called, then its declaration may be taken from another unit (see 12.5).

Examples:

```
unit sum: function (s: function (i:INTEGER):REAL; n:INTEGER):REAL;
  begin
    RESULT:=0;
    for i:=1 to n
    do
        RESULT:=RESULT+s(i)
    od
end sum;


unit q: function (i:INTEGER):REAL;
  begin
    RESULT:=1.0/REAL(i)**2
end q;

unit square_equation: procedure (a,b,c:REAL; output x1,x2:REAL);
    var delta: REAL;
  begin
    a:=2*a; c:=2*c;
    delta:=b**2−a*c;
    if delta<0 then write("no real roots"); return fi;
    if delta=0 then x1:=−b/a; x2:=x1; return fi;
    delta:=sqrt(delta);
    if b=0 then x1:=delta/a; x2:=−x1; return fi;
    if b>0 then b:=−b−delta else b:=−b+delta fi;
    x1:=b/a; x2:=c/b
end square_equation;
```

10.2. Subprogram Call

A subprogram call is either a *procedure call* or a *function call*. There are also some special kinds of *procedure calls* used in parallel computations, i.e. an *alien call* (see 16.2) and a *send statement* (see 16.3).

A *procedure call* is a statement, a *function call* is an expression. The value of this expression is defined by means of the predefined variable RESULT (see 10.1). Its type is the same as the corresponding *function type*.

<procedure call>::= <subprogram call>
<function call>::= <subprogram call>
<subprogram call>::= <subprogram name> <actual parameter list>
<subprogram name>::= <name>
References:
<actual parameter list> --> 9, <name> --> 6.1

The called subprogram may be either a declared subprogram, a variable of a *subprogram type* (see 5.1) or a formal parameter of another unit (see 9). When a subprogram is called its instance is generated.

Termination of a subprogram instance takes place when the *return statement* is executed or the corresponding sequence of statements is exhausted. It involves the same actions as in the case of other units (see 3.4). Moreover the instance of a subprogram (and all contained instances, if a subprogram inherits another unit, see 12) is deallocated.

Examples:

```
eps:= sum(q,1000)−sum(q,100);
square_equation( 3.27,−10.3,4.35,x,y);      −− where x,y are variables
```

11. Classes

A *class declaration* follows the form of a unit declaration (see 3.2).

<class head>::= { <inheritance part> }? **class** <formal parameter list>

References:

<inheritance part> --> 12, <formal parameter list> --> 9.1

A *class declaration* serves also as a *type declaration* (see 4.5.1). So, every *class* may be treated as a unit as well as a *type*. The first meaning is necessary for *class instance generation* (see 4.5.1.2) and the latter for *type definition* (see 4).

Class declaration associates identifier with a class (see 3.2). When this class is designated by applied occurrence of its identifier in a simple name (6.1.1) or in a binding name (6.1.4), then this name can be treated as both: a *class unit name* or a *class type name*. However for dotted names only one interpretation is possible (see 4.5.1.1).

A *class instance* generated by a *class generator* is an object of this class, i.e. it may be referred to by references. However, if class is inherited by another unit, then the corresponding *class instance* is not an object (see 12), but a part of an object.

An object of a class can be copied using a *copy operator* (4.5.3) and a useless object may be deallocated using *kill statement* (4.5.4).

Attributes of a *class object* may be accessed from outside of an object via dotted names, attributes of a *class type* are accessible from outside of a class via dotted names as well (see 6.1.3).

In each class there is function MY_CLASS predefined as a local entity. The value of this function is of the type of the declared class and it is the reference to the *class object* in whose the called MY_CLASS is a local entity (see 14). Function MY_CLASS cannot be used in subprograms and blocks inheriting classes (see 12).

Examples:

```
unit complex: class (re,im:REAL);
    var module: REAL;
  begin
    module := sqrt(re*re+im*im)
end complex;

{ push−down store }

unit Push_down: class (size: INTEGER);

    var STACK: arrayof OBJECT;
    top: INTEGER(=1);

unit push: procedure (x: OBJECT);
  begin
    if top>size
    then
        writeln (" stack overflow")
    else
        STACK[top] := x;
        top := top + 1;
    fi
end push;

unit pop: function :OBJECT;
  begin
    if top <= 1
    then
        writeln (" empty stack")
    else
        top := top − 1;
        RESULT := STACK[top]
    fi
end pop;

begin
    STACK := new array [1..size];
end Push_down;
```

{ The example of applications of Push_down }

```
unit account: class (name:STRING; value:REAL);
end account;
var store1, store2, store3: Push_down; n:INTEGER;
    a1,a2,a3: account;
        ...
    store1:=new Push_down(1000); store2:=new Push_down(200);
    store3:=new Push_down(n);
        ...
    a1:=new account("Smith",123.45);
    a2:=new account("Brown",245.50);
        ...
    store1.push(a1); store2.push(a2);
    a3:=store2.pop; store3.push(a3);
        { etc. }
```

12. Inheritance

12.1. Inheritance Sequences

<inheritance part>::= **inherits** <unit identifier>
References:
<unit identifier> --> 3.2

The occurrence of an inheritance part in a unit declaration (see 3.2, 8) causes that this declared unit inherits a unit determined by a unit identifier specified in this inheritance part. Only a *class*, a *coroutine* or a *process* may be inherited by another unit. Every unit may inherit a class. An inherited unit is determined in a unit specification (see 8) except blocks. For blocks the inheritance part should precede the keyword **block** (see 13). A coroutine and a process may not be inherited by a subprogram and a block.

A unit inherits all the properties of the inherited unit, if any.

Examples:

    Car: **class** (license_no: INTEGER);
    { specification of a class without inheritance part }
    Bus: **inherits** Car **class** (seats: INTEGER);
    { class Bus has its own properties andall properties of class Car }
    Mercedes_Benz_D: **inherits** Bus **class** (brand: STRING);
    { class Mercedes_Benz_D has its ownproperties and all properties of classBus (and
        thus it has also all propertiesof class Car) }

An inheritance sequence of unit M is the sequence of units M1,...,Mn, where Mn is M and, for i=1,...,n−1, unit Mi is inherited by Mi+1 and M1 inherits no unit. This sequence must be always finite. Hence recursion in the inheritance sequence is not allowed, i.e. one unit cannot appear more than once in such a sequence. Unit M inherits all the units M1,...,Mn−1 from its inheritance sequence.

If unit M inherits unit M', then any reference value to an object of M belongs to the type defined by M' (see 4.5.1). The set of values of the type defined by M is contained in the set of values of the type defined by M'. Class M defines in that sense a subtype of M', analogous to a discrete subtype (see 4.2.2).

An instance of a unit contains an instance of an inherited one, if any. This rule is applied inductively to the whole inheritance sequence. If an instance is not contained in any other instance, then it is called a maximal one. A maximal instance of a *class*, a *coroutine* or a *process* with all contained instances is called an object. Its execution is defined by means of the execution of statements of its contained instances (see 12.4)

Examples:

```
var B1, B2: Bus;
    M1, M2, M3: Mercedes_Benz_D;
B1 := new Bus(13200, 32);
B2 := new Mercedes_Benz_D(14200, 36, "0303/11R");
M1 := new Mercedes_Benz_D(16000, 40, "0303/12R");
M2 := none;
M3 := new Bus(16000, 40);
            -- incorrect, M3 is of type Mercedes_Benz_D
            -- and may not denote to an object of Bus
```

If a *coroutine* (a *process*) occurs in an inheritance sequence of a unit, then this unit is treated as a *coroutine* (a *process* respectively). Every *process* may be treated as a *coroutine* as well (see 16.1).

12.2. Membership Operators

The language introduces two boolean operators concerning inheritance (see 6.2.3).

      <membership operator>::= **in** | **is**

In the relation X **in** S, X is an expression denoting an object and S is a *type name* (see 4) denoting a *class*, a *coroutine* or *process type*. The type of an expression X must be consistent with S (see 4.7). If the value of X does not belong to the set of values determined by type S, then the value of the relation X **in** S is FALSE. Otherwise it is TRUE.

In the relation X **is** S, X is an expression denoting an object and S is a *type name* denoting a *class*, a *coroutine* or *process type*. The type of an expression X must be consistent with S (see 4.7). The value of the relation X **is** S is TRUE iff the value of the expression X is the reference to an object of the class denoted by *type name* S.

Examples:

```
{ for B1, B2, M1 and M2 defined as in the previous example }
B1 in Bus                  -- TRUE
B2 in Car                  -- TRUE
M2 is Mercedes_Benz_D      -- FALSE
B2 in Mercedes_Benz_D      -- TRUE
M1 is Bus                  -- FALSE
M1 in Bus                  -- TRUE
M2 in Bus                  -- TRUE
```

12.3. Concatenation of Local Entities

The local entities of a unit without inheritance part are the entities declared in this unit (see 3.3 and 9).

The local entities of a unit are the entities declared in this unit and the local entities of the inherited unit, if any. In that sense the entities declared within the unit are concatenated to the inherited entities. The only exception are virtual subprograms (see 12.5).

Examples:

```
unit Car: class (license_no: INTEGER);
    var dead_weight: REAL
        -- local entities: license_no, dead_weight
end Car;
unit Bus: inherits Car class (seats: INTEGER):
        -- local entities: license_no, dead_weight,
        -- seats
end Bus;
unit Lorry: inherits Car class;
    var capacity: REAL
        -- local entities: license_no, dead_weight,
        -- capacity
end Lorry;
unit Mercedes_Benz_D: inherits Bus class (brand: STRING);
        -- local entities: license_no, dead_weight,
        -- seats, brand
end Mercedes_Benz_D;
```

With the use of inheritance, tree structured hierarchies of units may be constructed. For instance, in the above example:

```
                Car
              .   .
            .       .
          .           .
        Bus         Lorry
          .
          .
          .
     Mercedes_Benz_D
```

Formal parameters (see 9) are also concatenated, i.e. the formal parameters of a unit are the formal parameters declared in the unit head as well as the formal parameters of the inherited unit, if any. Consequently, in an instance generator of a unit the actual parameter list must correspond to the concatenated list of formal parameters.

Examples:

    B1 := **new** Bus(13200, 32);
    M1 := **new** Mercedes_Benz_D(12800, 37, "0303/9R");

12.4. Concatenation of Statements

The unit instance execution consists in the execution of the concatenated sequence of statements from all units of its inheritance sequence. The concatenation of statements is performed by means of an *inner statement.*

    <inner statement>::= **inner**

The *inner statement* may occur at most once in a *class body* but not in any nested block. Nevertheless, it may be executed many times (e.g. in a loop statement). When the *inner statement* does not occur explicitly in the body, it is assumed to be its last statement (before *lastwill statements* — for *lastwill statements* and their concatenation see 17.1.4).

Let M be a unit and M1,...,Mn=M be its inheritance sequence. The execution of an instance of M starts with the first statement of the body of M1. Then, for i from 1 to n−1, when the *inner statement* is encountered in the body of unit Mi, the statements of Mi+1 body are executed instead of this *inner statement.* The *inner statement* in the body of M is executed as an empty statement.

When the list of statements of M1 is exhausted, the termination of the instance of unit M takes place. The termination may also appear as a result of the execution of *return statement* in any moment of the execution of sequence M1,...,Mn. The final parameter transmission is performed upon a unit instance termination (see 9). After these actions the unit instance becomes terminated, if M is a subprogram or a class. For the semantics of termination and *return statement* in *coroutines* consult 15 and in *processes* consult 16.

Examples:

```
    unit Bst: class; { binary search tree }
        unit member: inherits help function :BOOLEAN ->;
        unit insert: inherits help procedure ->;
        unit help: class (i:INTEGER); { auxiliary class }
        end help ->;
    end Bst ->;
    ->unit Bst: body;
        var root:node;
        unit node: class (value:INTEGER);
            var left,right:node;
        end node;
        ->unit help: class (i:INTEGER); { auxiliary class }
            var p,q:node;
          begin
            q:=root;
            while q=/= none
            do
                if i < q.value
                then
                        p:=q; q:=q.left; repeat
                fi;
                if q.value < i
                then
                        p:=q; q:=q.right; repeat
                fi;
                exit
            od;
            inner
        end help;
        ->unit member: inherits help function :BOOLEAN;
            { i here is a formal parameter derived from help }
          begin
            RESULT:=q=/=none
        end member;
        -> unit insert: inherits help procedure;
          begin
            if q=/=none then return fi;
            q:=new node(i);
            if p=none then root:=q; return fi;
            if p.value < i then p.right:=q else p.left:=q fi;
        end insert;
    end Bst;
```

12.5. Virtual Subprograms

A declaration of a subprogram in a specification part of a class is the special case of a subprogram declaration. This declaration introduces the so-called virtual subprogram. It means that if such a virtual subprogram is called, then its declaration may be taken from a unit inheriting this class.

When a virtual subprogram is declared as an entity of an inheriting unit, it is concatenated with the local entities of the inherited unit in a specific way. If a local entity of the inherited unit is a virtual subprogram associated (see 3.3) with the same identifier as the concatenated one, then this concatenated subprogram substitutes the inherited one. It is just like the redefinition of an existing virtual subprogram what is different from the inheritance rule applied to non-virtual entities (when the concatenation results in the two different local entities, although associated with the same identifier).

The substitution of a virtual subprogram is allowed only if the head of the new subprogram is semantically equivalent to the head of the inherited one (see 9.2).

A declaration of a virtual subprogram as a local entity of a class defines its meaning only tentatively. This meaning may be later redefined by any unit which inherits (see 12.1) this class. Thus the final meaning of a virtual subprogram is not set up at the moment of its declaration but rather at the moment of the generation of a unit with this virtual subprogram as a local entity. This mechanism is similar to the substitution of a formal parameter by an actual one (see 9). The tentative virtual definition may be considered as the "default value" for an actual subprogram.

If a virtual inherited subprogram is not redeclared in a unit, then its meaning is defined as in the inherited class. However the declaration of another entity with the same identifier as a virtual inherited subprogram in a specification part of a unit covers the meaning of such a virtual subprogram, as in the case of a normal entity.

Examples:

```
unit A : class;
    var i: INTEGER;
    unit proc: procedure; . . . end proc;
body;
    ...
end A;
```

unit B : **inherits** A **class**;
    var i:INTEGER;
    unit proc: **procedure**; . . . **end** proc;
body;
    ...
end B;

unit C : **inherits** B **class**;
    var i:INTEGER;
body;
    ...
end C;

unit D : **inherits** B **class**;
    var i:INTEGER;
    proc: REAL;
body;
    ...
end D;

var X : A; Y: D;

begin

    X := **new** C;
    Y := **new** D;
    A(X).i   −− denotes variable i declared in A
    A(X).proc   −− THIS IS SUBPROGRAM FROM B !!!
    B(X).i   −− denotes variable i declared in B
    B(X).proc   −− denotes virtual subprogram proc declared in B
    X.i   −− denotes variable i declared in A
    X.proc   −− denotes virtual subprogram proc declared in B
{ The declaration of procedure proc from B had substituted that from A, when the
  object X was generated }

    Y.i   −− denotes variable i declared in D
    Y.proc   −− denotes variable proc declared in D
    B(Y).i   −− denotes variable i declared in B
    B(Y).proc   −− denotes virtual subprogram proc declared in B
    A(Y).i   −− denotes variable i declared in A
    A(Y).proc   −− denotes virtual subprogram proc declared in B

13. Blocks

Block is a unit which requires no declaration; it stands for a statement. Consequently, it may appear only in the sequence of statements of another unit or as the outermost unit, in which case it is called a main block or a program. The execution of a *block statement* consists in the generation and the execution of a *block instance* (see 3.4).

<block>::= {<block identifier> : }? {**block** <unit body> |
  {<inherited class>{{<executive part> <end part>}|{**block** <unit body>}}} }
<inherited class>::= **inherits** <class identifier> <actual parameter list>
<block identifier>::= <unit identifier>
References:
<class identifier> --> 11, <actual parameter list> --> 9
<executive part> --> 7, <end part> --> 8
<unit body> --> 8.1, <unit identifier> --> 3.2

A block may be named, and then, the *block identifier* may appear before the beginning of a block and may optionally follow the corresponding *end symbol*.

A block may inherit a class. The instance of such a block contains the instance of this class. All the other rules concerning inheritance are valid in the case of such a block (see 12). During a *block instance generation* an actual parameter list is associated with the formal parameter list inherited from inherited class (see 9). For a normal block the actual parameter list is empty.

If an inherited class is present and a declarative part is empty, then the block may start immediately from the executive part. Otherwise a block must start from the keyword **block**.

When a *block instance* is terminated, it is deallocated as in the case of subprograms (see 10.2). If a block inherits a class, then all contained instances are also simultaneously deallocated.

Main block may be treated as *coroutine* and a *process* as well (see 15, 16). There is a predefined function MAIN the value of which may be used as the reference to *coroutine* or *process* (when required) in *coroutine or process operations*. However no *class operation* e.g. *kill* or *copy* may be applied to this value.

Examples:

```
Main_block:
block
    var n:INTEGER;
begin
    read (n);
    for i:=1 to n
    do
        block            -- anonymous nested block
            var a, b, c, p, S:REAL;
        begin
            read (a, b, c);
            p:=(a+b+c)/2;
            S:=sqrt(p*(p−a)*(p−b)*(p−c));
            write (S);
            writeln (i:10);
        end;
    od;
end Main_block;


inherits push_down(1000)
begin
    inherits Bst
    begin
{ An example of two nested blocks inheriting classes. Herein both data structures
  push_down andBst are directly accessible.  }
    end;
end
```

14. Identifier Binding Rules

Every applied occurrence of an identifier (see 2.2) must be uniquely bound to an entity which is designated by it. Binding rules are static. They remain unchanged for run time, providing that the notion of a unit is replaced by the notion of an instance (see 3.4).

The simplest case of an identifier binding rule concerns local entities of a given unit (see 14.1). The concept of accessibility scope makes this binding dependent on the place ("view-point") where the identifier is applied. Designating local entities is merely a helpful auxiliary notion which is, however, not powerful enough to define real binding.

Identifiers may be applied within names only (see 6.1). Section 14.2 uses the notions introduced in section 14.1 in order to define the binding rules for applied occurrences of identifiers within an arbitrary form of a name.

14.1. Designating the Local Entities of a Unit

For every applied occurrence of an identifier its context determines a unit where for the corresponding local entity (see 3.3 and 14.2) should be searched. This searching algorithm involves only entities accessible from the considered applied occurrence ("view-point").

The accessibility scope of a declared entity is the unit body most tightly enclosing its declaration (see 8.1). An identifier associated with this entity (see 3.3) may be applied within its accessibility scope.

If an entity associated with the applied occurrence of an identifier is declared in a unit inheriting no other unit, then the uniqueness of identifiers association with entities (see 3.3) defines uniquely the required entity. For a unit inheriting another unit the concatenation of local entities (see 12.3) may lead to ambiguous associations. In this case the entity declared within an inheriting unit takes precedence over any local entity of an inherited unit. However, this covered entity may still be accessed by qualified names (6.3) or binding names (6.1.4).

Since the association algorithm considers accessibility of local entities only, any association conflict with a non-accessible local entity is not significant.

14.2. Direct and Indirect Binding

Identifiers which are used to designate local entities in forms of dotted names (6.1.3) or binding names (6.1.4) are bound indirectly. Simple names (6.1.1) and remaining applied occurrences of identifiers (see 2.2) are bound directly.

In the case of indirect binding the corresponding name defines a unit whose local entity is to be designated by the applied occurrence of an identifier. The proper entity is then found according to the rules given in 14.1.

In the case of direct binding, the searching must be done for the proper local entity of the unit most tightly enclosing the given applied occurrence. If it fails, then the searching is repeated for units successively enclosing the innermost one. For correct programs this rule should always establish a unit with local entity designated by the given identifier and most tightly enclosing its applied occurrence.

At run time, instead of units the corresponding unit instances are pointed for non-local entities association. All these instances form the environment of the currently executed instance.

Examples:

```
block var x: C; i: INTEGER;
    unit C: class; var r: REAL; i: INTEGER;
        begin . . .
            r:=i        -- both local variables of C
                        -- i from C takes precedence over i from the outer block
            x.r         -- dotted name of variable r from an object denoted by
                        -- variable x from the outer block
        end C;
    begin . . .
        i               -- local variable of block
        r               -- incorrect, this occurrence of identifier r may not be
                        -- bound to any program entity
        x:=new C        -- local variable x is set to the reference of
                        -- the newly generated object of class C,
                        -- C denotes class declared in this block
        x.r             -- dotted name designating variable r from the generated
                        -- object of class C
    end
```

```
block var X: D;
    unit C: class; var b: BOOLEAN;
    end C;
    unit D: inherits C class; var b: BOOLEAN;
      begin
          b       -- local variable declared in D
          C'b     -- variable declared in C
      end D;

    unit F: inherits C function : INTEGER;
          var b: BOOLEAN;
          unit P: procedure;
              var i: INTEGER;
            begin
                i       -- local variable declared in P
                b       -- variable declared in F
                C'b     -- variable declared in class C
            end P;
          begin
              b         -- local variable declared in F
              C'b       -- variable declared in C
              X.b       -- an attribute of an object of class D
                        -- being a variable declared in D
              C(X).b    -- an attribute of the same object
                        -- being a variable declared in C
      end F;
          . . .
end
```

```
unit Library: class; var d: D;

    unit C: class; var x: INTEGER; end C ->;

    unit D: inherits C class; var y: INTEGER; end D ->;

    unit P: procedure;
      begin
        d.x   -- variable of an object of class D taken
              -- from inherited C
        d.y   -- variable of the same object taken from class D
        d.r   -- incorrect, this attribute of C is invisible here
      end P;

body

    -> unit C: class; var r: REAL; end C;

    ->unit D: inherits C class; var x: BOOLEAN; end D;

  begin
    d.x        -- boolean variable from class D
    d.y        -- integer variable from class D
    d.r        -- real variable of an object of class D taken
               -- from class C
end Library;
```

15. Coroutines

15.1. Coroutine Declaration and Generation

Coroutines allow programmed multiplexing inside one *process*. A *coroutine declaration* follows the form of a unit declaration (see 3.2).

<coroutine head>::= {<inheritance part>}? **coroutine** <formal parameter list>
References:
<inheritance part> --> 12, <formal parameter list> --> 9.1

A unit declared as a *coroutine* may be considered simultaneously as a *coroutine* and a *class*. A *coroutine instance* is generated by a *class generator* (see 4.5.1.2). The generation of a *coroutine instance* implies the generation of the corresponding *coroutine object*, as in the case of *classes* (see 11 and 12).

When a *coroutine instance* is generated by a *class generator*, then the corresponding *class instance* is generated, i.e. all the actions concerning *class instance* generation are performed (see 4.5.1.2, 11). A *coroutine object generation* is completed successfully only if a *return statement* was encountered during a *coroutine instance generation*. Otherwise the result of the corresponding *class generator* is a *class object*, not a *coroutine object*.

When a *return statement* was encountered during a *coroutine object generation*, then the *coroutine instance* becomes suspended at the statement just following such a *return statement*. The generated *coroutine object* becomes suspended at the same point. Then, as for *class object* termination, the final parameter transmission is performed (see 9) and the execution of an instance which generated that *coroutine object* is continued.

15.2. Coroutine Control Statements

<coroutine control statements>::= <attach statement> |
<exceptional coroutine statement>
<attach statement>::= **attach** (<expression>)
References:
<exceptional coroutine statement> --> 17.2, <expression> --> 6.2

Coroutine control statements are used for mutually exclusive activation of *coroutine objects*. Only such a statement can suspend the execution of an active *coroutine object* and activate another one. Thus if the execution of a *coroutine instance* is suspended by the generation of any other instance, then the active *coroutine object* is considered to be still executed.

The value of an expression given as a parameter of an *attach statement* must be a reference to a suspended *coroutine object*, otherwise the system signal Attach_Error is raised. The same signal is raised when this parameter determines an active or terminated (see 15.3) *coroutine object*.

If the parameter of an *attach statement* determines a *suspended coroutine object*, then the execution of this *coroutine object* is continued while the execution of the *current coroutine object* is suspended.

A *coroutine object* (which is not a *process*, cf. 16.4) may be deallocated by the *kill statement* only if it is suspended or terminated. Otherwise such a *kill statement* raises the signal Kill_Error. The deallocation of a *suspended coroutine object* includes the deallocation of all non-terminated instances of subprograms, blocks and classes which were generated during the execution of this *coroutine instance*. Finally, the *coroutine object* is deallocated as in the case of terminated *class object* (see 4.5.4).

The predefined function MY_COROUTINE of type OBJECT returns the reference to a *coroutine object* which evaluates this function.

There is also a predefined function LAST_ATTACH returning the reference to that *coroutine object* which as the last one performed an *attach statement*.

Examples:

The typical cooperation of two coroutines is presented. One reads a sequence of real numbers, another one prints these numbers, n per line. The input stream ends with 0.0.

```
block
    var prod: producer; cons: consumer; n: INTEGER;
        item: REAL; last: BOOLEAN;
    unit producer: coroutine;
      begin
        return;
        do
            read (item);           { item is a common variable }
            if item = 0.0 then last := TRUE fi; attach (cons)
        od
    end producer;
    unit consumer: coroutine ( n:INTEGER);
        var buff: arrayof REAL; j:INTEGER;
      begin
        buff := new array [1..n]
        return;
        do
            for i := 1 to n
            do
                if last then j:=i; exit exit fi; buff[i] := item;
                attach ( prod)
            od;
            for i := 1 to n           { print buffer }
            do
                write (' ', buff[i])
            od; writeln
        od;
        if j>0          { print the rest of buffer }
        then
            for i := 1 to j do write (' ', buff[i]) od;
            writeln;
        fi;
        attach (LAST_ATTACH)
    end consumer;
begin
    prod := new producer; read (n);
    cons := new consumer(n); attach (prod)
end
```

15.3. Coroutine Object Termination

A *suspended coroutine object* may be reactivated by an *attach statement*. When a *reactivated coroutine instance* executes a *return statement* or its sequence of statements ends, then that *coroutine instance* and the corresponding *coroutine object* become terminated.

Coroutine object termination forces signal raising, since this situation is treated as an exceptional one (see 17.1). Thus the system signal Cor_Term (*coroutine terminated*) is raised to another *coroutine object* by exceptional *coroutine statement* (see 17.2). The *coroutine object* to which this signal is raised is defined by the value of variable LAST_ATTACH (the last *coroutine* which caused the reactivation of the terminated one). If this value is equal to **none** , then the specified signal is raised to coroutine MY_PROCESS, which must be non-empty.

16. Processes

The language provides some facilities for defining concurrent computations. The fundamental notion is that of a *process*. *Process* is a kind of an object which defines sequential computation. A concurrent program consists of a number of cooperating *processes*. The *main block* is a distinguished process which is activated by an operating system, all other processes are generated and controlled by the user.

A *process*, i.e. an object of a unit specified by the keyword **process**, is generated similarly as a *coroutine object* (see 15.1). For the details of *process generation* consult 16.1.

Processes may share common stores or may be distributed. Both ways of concurrent computations are accepted in the language.

If a process generates another process without definition of a node number in a computer network (see 16.1), then it is assumed that the generated process is allocated in the same store as the generating one.

If a process generates another process and a node number in a computer network is specified in a process generator (see 16.1), then the distributed system of processes comes into play. These two processes are executed by two different connected computers. The language does not predict any special topology for a considered computer network neither the character of communication protocols.

The communication between processes may be synchronous or asynchronous. Synchronous communication is provided by *alien calls* (see 16.2), asynchronous communication is provided by *send statements* (see 16.3).

The communication between processes need not to be performed only by *alien calls* or by *send statements*. If processes share a common store, they may communicate also with the use of shared data. The language does not define, however, what happens when more than one process change simultaneously the value of such a common data. Moreover, when a distributed process attempts to access a data not belonging to its local store, e.g. via a reference to an object from another store or via a visible entity allocated in another store etc., then the system signal Acc_Error is raised (see 17.3).

The predefined function MY_PROCESS of type OBJECT returns the reference to the process which evaluates this function.

16.1. Process Declaration and Generation

\<process head\>::= {\<inheritance part\>}? **process** \<formal parameter list\>
\<process generator\>::= \<class generator\> { **at** \<expression\> }?
References:
\<inheritance part\> −−\> 12, \<formal parameter list\> −−\> 9.1
\<class generator\> −−\> 4.5.1.2, \<expression\> −−\> 6.2

A unit declared as a process may be considered simultaneously as a process and a coroutine (see 15.1). The objects of a process are generated in a similar way as the objects of a coroutine. There are, however, two forms of process generation. If a *process generator* has the same form as a *class generator*, then a new process is generated in the same store as the generating process. If the keyword **at** followed by an expression appears after the *class generator*, then the value of this expression defines a node number in a computer network. The type of this expression must be integer and its value must define an existing node in the network. In such a case this new process is generated in the indicated node.

The generation of a local process as well as a distributed one is performed by a generating process. It creates a new object, transmits *input parameters* and starts to execute the corresponding sequence of statements. When a *return statement* is reached, the final parameter transmission is performed and the execution of the process generator terminates. Then both processes, i.e. the generating process and the generated process continue their computations.

If no *return statement* is encountered during a process generation, then a new process is not successfully generated. In the case of a local process generation, the generated object is treated as an object of a class, as in the case of a coroutine generation (see 15.1). In the case of a distributed process the generated object is immediately deallocated, so the returned value of the process generator is **none** .

The newly generated object of a process may be also treated as an *active coroutine object*, until it performs an *attach statement*. This coroutine object may be attached only by another coroutine object executed by this process.

Examples:

        unit Semaphore: **process** (n: INTEGER);
        ...
        end Semaphore;
        var X,Y: Semaphore;
        X:= **new** Semaphore(2);   −− Semaphore X is a local process
        Y:= **new** Semaphore(1) **at** 1;   −− Semaphore Y is a distributed process

16.2. Process Communication by Alien Calls

<alien call>::= **alien** <procedure call>
<communication statement>::= <enable statement> | <disable statement> |
   <accept statement> | <return from alien call>
<enable statement>::= **enable** { <name> ♯ ,}⁺
<disable statement>::= **disable** { <name> ♯ ,}⁺
<accept statement>::= **accept** { <name> ♯.,}* { **timeout** <expression> }?
<return from alien call>::= **return** { <disable statement> }? { <enable statement> }?
References:
<procedure call> −−> 10.2, <name> −−> 6.1

Any procedure declared in a specification part of a process may be used for process communication. Such a communication procedure may be called by remote access in an *alien
call statement.* Hence a *procedure name* appearing in an *alien call* must be of the form of
a dotted name (see 6.1.3).

The value of an expression appearing before a dot determines a *process object* which is the
receiver. A *calling process*, which is the sender, waits until the execution of a communication procedure is completed. The execution of that procedure is performed by the receiver.
When the execution of a communication procedure is terminated, both processes continue
their computations. The transmission of parameters is executed as in a *normal procedure
call.*

In the case of an *alien call*, when a receiver is not well-defined (i.e. it is not *process object*
see 16.1 or it is the sender), then the system signal Comm_Error is raised (see 17.3).

Alien calls are controlled in a receiver by a system of masks. An *alien call* may take
place only if the mask of a called procedure is open for a communication. After a new
process generation all its communication procedures, if any, are closed for a communication.
During a process execution the state of a mask may be changed with the use of *enable* or
disable statement.

The execution of an *enable statement* causes that all procedures appearing on the list
become open for a communication. If there are already some procedures open for a communication, then after the execution of an *enable statement* they remain open for a communication.

The execution of a *disable statement* causes that all procedures appearing on the list become closed for a communication. The procedures open for a communication not belonging
to this list remain open for a communication.

If a communication procedure is open and an *alien call* was executed, then the communication between processes may take place. A sender waits always for the termination of an *alien call*, but a receiver does not wait for such a communication. It may be interrupted by an *alien call*, if the corresponding procedure is open for a communication. The moment of such an interrupt is arbitrary. Moreover the language does not precise the way of choice between different possible communications. On the other hand it is assumed that the strategy of choice is strongly fair.

If a communication procedure is closed for a communication, then a sender waits until it becomes open.

Upon the entrance into a communication procedure all procedures of the receiver become closed for a communication.

The termination of an *alien call* takes place when in a communication procedure a *return statement* is encountered or when its sequence of statements ends. In such a case the masks in a receiver are restored to the state from before the call. Another way of the termination of an *alien call* is provided by the special form of *return statement* (return from *alien call*). This kind of statement is allowed only within a communication procedure and may be used when the termination of a communication requires some simultaneous changes in the state of masks. If a return from *alien call* has non-empty list of *enabled procedures* and/or non-empty list of *disabled procedures*, then the execution of such a *return* implies the changes on the restored state of masks in a receiver according to the *enable* and *disable lists*.

A more synchronized way of communication is provided by *accept statement*. In this case not only a sender waits for the termination of an *alien call* but also a receiver waits for the termination of an *accept statement*. When an *accept statement* is executed by a receiver, all procedures appearing on the list become open for a communication, in addition to those already open. After a successful communication all procedures from the list become closed for a communication, except those open prior to the execution of the *accept statement*.

Accept statement with a *timeout part* provides a way for real time programming. An expression appearing in the *timeout part* must be of type REAL. Its value determines the period of time (counted in seconds) after which the execution of the *accept statement* is terminated, successfully or not.

The execution of a communication statement is indivisible, i.e. the execution of such a statement by a receiver may not be interrupted by another process.

The communication by means of *alien calls* is synchronized in a receiver with the use of masks. The language does not define the general strategy for scheduling different *alien calls* in a receiver. In order to enable a proper way of scheduling, a predefined function PENDING of type integer is provided. An actual parameter of this function must be a name of a communication procedure. The returned value is the number of not yet handled *alien calls* to such a communication procedure.

Examples:

```
unit Semaphore : process (n:INTEGER);
    unit P: procedure ;
    { implements operation P(S) }
    begin
        n:=n-1;
        if n=0
        then
            return disable P
        fi;
    end P;
    unit V: procedure ;
    { implements operation V(S) }
    begin
        n:=n+1;
        return enable P
    end V;
begin
    return;
    enable V;
    { procedure V is always open for a communication}
    if n>0
    then
        enable P;
        { procedure P is open if n>0}
    fi;
    do
        { waiting loop for a communication }
        accept
    od;
end Semaphore;
var S:Semaphore;


    ...
    S:=new Semaphore(1);   -- generates a new semaphore
    ...
    alien S.P;             -- executes P(S)
    ...                    -- critical region
    alien S.V;             -- executes V(S)
```

16.3. Process Communication by Send Statements

<send statement>::= **send** <procedure call>
References:
<procedure call> --> 10.2

Send statement serves for asynchronous communication between processes. Syntactically it has a similar form to *alien call*. A procedure called by such a statement must be a communication procedure. A process executing this statement is a sender. A process appearing in the corresponding dotted name is a receiver.

When a *send statement* is executed, a sender does not wait for the termination of a communication. The actions of a receiver are defined as in the case of an *alien call*. So such a communication procedure must not have *output parameters*. Moreover, if a receiver is not well-defined (see 16.2), a *send statement* does not force any signal raising (contrary to the case of *alien call*).

Examples:

```
    unit Spooler: process ;
    var
            Q: queue;
            f:filename;


        unit print: procedure (f:filename);
        begin
            Q.insert(f);
            if Q.full
            then
                    return disable print
            fi ;
        end print;
```

```
begin
    Q:= new queue;
    return;
    do
        disable print;
        if Q.empty
        then
            accept print
        fi;
        f:=Q.delete;
        enable print;
        { write file f }
    od;
end Spooler;


var S:Spooler;


    ...
    S:=new Spooler;    -- generates a Spooler
    ...
    send S.print;      -- asynchronous call of procedure print
    ...
```

16.4. Process Termination and Deallocation

The termination of a distributed process differs substantially from the termination of a local process.

When a local process encounters a *return statement* or its sequence of statements ends, such a process becomes to be terminated. From that moment its object is treated as an object of a class, i.e. all attributes of such a terminated process may be used by remote access. The explicit deallocation of such an object by means of *kill statement* is allowed.

When a distributed process encounters a *return statement* or its sequence of statements ends, such a process becomes to be terminated. From that moment its object does not exist, i.e. it is automatically deallocated. An attempt to access its attributes is illegal, i.e. the system signal Acc_Error will be raised.

17. Exception Handling

The language provides some facilities for dealing with errors and other exceptional situations that may arise at run time. This chapter contains a description of exception handling in sequential, semi-parallel (*coroutine*) and parallel computations.

17.1. Exception Handling in Sequential Computations

In the sequential part of the language an exceptional event called "exception" causes a suspension of normal program execution. Detection of an exception is expressed by raising a *signal*. Executing some actions in response to an exception occurrence is called signal handling.

Signal identifiers are introduced by *signal declaration*. *Signals* can be raised by *raise statements*, or alternatively they are raised because of a run-time error. When an exception arises, the control can be passed to a user-pointed handler associated with the raised signal. The principles of determining a handler that responds to the raised signal are presented in 17.1.3.

17.1.1. Signal Declaration

<signal declaration>::=
    signal {<signal identifier> <formal parameter list> ♮ ,}$^+$;
<signal identifier>::= <identifier>
References:
<identifier> --> 2.2, <formal parameter list> --> 9.1

The *signal declaration* defines signals which can appear in *raise statements* and in *signal handlers* within the scope of the declaration. The identifiers of *system signals*, i.e. signals associated with run-time errors, are not specified in the signal declaration.

17.1.2. Signal Handlers

A *signal handler* is a list of statements that are intended to be processed when a signal is raised.

\<exceptions declaration\>::= **exceptions** {\<exception when part\>}⁺

\<exception when part\>::= **when** {\<signal name\> ♯ ,}⁺ {\<formal parameter list\>}? :
    \<sequence of statements\>

\<signal name\>::= \<name\>

References:

\<name\> --\> 6.1, \<sequence of statements\> --\> 7

\<formal parameter list\> --\> 9.1

An *exceptions declaration* may appear in the declarative part of a unit as the last declaration, i.e. once just before the keyword **begin**, if present. Any exception when part is associated with one or more signals. The sequence of statements appearing after a colon define a particular handler responding to these signals. If such a handler does not specify formal parameter list, then every associated signal must specify formal parameter list semantically equivalent (see 9.2) to the list specified by each other. Moreover, the corresponding parameters should be declared with exactly the same identifiers. If a formal parameter list is specified in a handler, then semantic equivalence of this list and each of the lists specified for the corresponding signals is sufficient. A handler in an exception when part can handle only named signals.

Any statement (except *inner statement*) whose occurrence in a unit is legal may occur in a handler declared within this unit. All identifiers visible in the unit and the signal formal parameter lists may be used in the handler statements.

Examples:

```
exceptions
     when emptytree: T:=new treelem; return;
     when overflow: raise Arithmetic_Error;
```

17.1.3. Signal Raising

A signal can be raised explicitly by a *raise statement* or implicitly as a result of a run-time error occurrence.

<raise statement>::= {**raise** <signal name> <actual parameter list>

References:

<signal name> --> 17.1.2, <actual parameter list> --> 9

Examples:

> **raise** empty(exprstack);
> **raise** end_of_file (input);

When a signal is raised, the normal computations are suspended, a handler instance is allocated and then executed. The actual parameters are transmitted to the handler instance, as in the case of a procedure (see 9). However, the crucial point of exception handling is the way in which such a handler is searched for and how it is activated.

Suppose that the instance P of unit M raises signal f. If the signal f is raised during the execution of *lastwill statements* in the instance P (see 17.1.4) then the program abnormally terminates. If a handler f is a local entity of M, then that handler is activated. In all the other cases the following actions are performed:

(1) if M is a class, block, function or procedure, then signal f is propagated to the instance which has generated the instance of M; this does not concern the case when instance of M is in the state of executing its *lastwill statements* (see 17.1.4).

(2) if M is a signal handler, then the signal f is propagated to the instance P' of the unit containing this handler as a local entity; however, the instance P' is treated as if it would contain no handlers as local entities; note that the *raise statement* occurring in a handler cannot cause the activation of any handler contained within the same instance;

(3) if M is a coroutine, then the system signal Hand_Not_Found is raised to MY_PROCESS (see 15.3);

(4) if M is a program (process), then the program (process) terminates.

The propagation of the signal to the unit instance causes searching for a handler as if the signal was raised at the resumption point of this instance.

In an instance of a unit with non-empty inheritance part, a handler declared in the inheriting unit is covered by the handler declared in the inherited unit, if present. Thus a signal raised during the execution of the inherited statements can be handled by a handler declared in the inherited unit.

Examples:

```
first:block
      signal f;
      unit A: procedure;
        begin
             .....
           raise f                  -- handler H1 or H2 is executed, according
             .....                  -- to the invocation point of A
        end A;
      unit B: procedure;
         exceptions
              when f: .....;        -- handler H1
         begin
           A;                       -- if f is raised, handler H1 is activated
           raise f;                 -- causes the activation of handler H1
             .....
        end B;
      exceptions
           when f: .....;           -- handler H2
      begin
        raise f;                    -- handler H2 is activated
        B;
          .....
        A;                          -- if f is raised, handler H2 is activated
      end first;
```

```
second: block
   signal f;
   unit A: class;
       signal g,h;
       exceptions
           when g: .... ;   —— handler G1
           when h: .... ;   —— handler H1
       unit p: procedure;
         begin

               .....
             raise g; .... raise h;
               .....
         end p;
       begin

           .....
         raise f;

           .....
         raise g;

           .....
   end A;

   unit B: inherits A class;
       exceptions
           when f: ... ;   —— handler F1
           when g: ... ;   —— handler G2
       begin
         raise f;

           .....
         raise g;

           .....
         raise h;

           .....
         p;

           .....
       end B;
   begin

         ......
end second;
```

If signal f or g is raised in an object of class B (or propagated to it by procedure p), the handler F1 and G2 is executed (respectively), even if signals are raised in the statements of class A; if signal h is raised, handler H1 is activated.

17.1.4. Handler Actions

A handler execution terminates if one of the exception control statements is executed.

<exception control statement>::= <return statement> | **terminate**
References:
<return statement> --> 7.1

The handler control statement *terminate* may appear only within a handler declaration. The execution of that statement causes the termination of the handler instance and the abnormal termination of the instance which raised the signal and of all instances which propagated it. If such a statement does not appear in the handler, then *return statement* is assumed to appear by default at the end of a handler sequence of statements. The execution of *return statement* has the similar effect as in a procedure, i.e. the control returns to the instance where the signal was raised and the execution of this instance is normally continued.

Sometimes an abnormal termination of instances by a *terminate statement* requires certain actions to be executed, e.g. it is necessary to release some storage, to close some files etc. *Lastwill statements* are provided for this aim.

<lastwill statements>::= **lastwill** <sequence of statements>
References:
<sequence of statements> --> 7

Any unit body may end with a sequence of statements following the keyword **lastwill**. These statements are executed before an abnormal termination of the instance. If *lastwill statements* do not appear in a unit, the corresponding empty statement will be executed. If an instance ends in the natural way, then *lastwill statements* are never executed. In an instance of the inheriting unit, the *lastwill statements* are processed successively, tracing the inheritance sequence in the reverse order. *Lastwill statements* cannot contain the *raise statement* (see 17.1.3). During the execution of *lastwill statements* no signal can be propagated to the instance executing them. However, signals can be raised and handled in all the instances generated during the execution of *lastwill statements*.

Let us consider a sequence of instances P1,...,Pn such that Pi+1 is generated by Pi (i=1,...,n-1) and Pi is a *process or coroutine instance*, and assume that signal f raised in the instance Pk is handled by handler H found in Pi (i < k).

The *return statement* executed in the handler H causes Pk to be normally continued. The control is passed to the statement just following the corresponding **raise f**.

The execution of a *terminate statement* causes the displacement of resumption points in the instances Pi,...,Pk to their *lastwill statements*. Then instance Pk is resumed as in the case of *return statement*. Thus *terminate statement* causes the termination and deallocation of instances Pi,...,Pk after executing their *lastwill statements*.

Examples:

```
block
    signal Wrong_data(t:STRING);
    unit square_equation: procedure (a,b,c:REAL; output x1,x2:REAL);
        var delta: REAL;
        exceptions
            when Num_Error:
                if a=0 and b=/=0
                then
                    x1:=-c/b; terminate
                else raise Wrong_data (" no roots")
                fi
        begin { Num_Error will be raised in the case of division by zero }
            a:=2*a; c:=2*c;
            delta:=b**2-a*c;
            if delta=0 then x1:=-b/a; x2:=x1; return fi;
            delta:=sqrt(delta);
            if b=0 then x1:=delta/a; x2:=-x1; return fi;
            if b>0 then b:=-b-delta else b:=-b+delta fi;
            x1:=b/a; x2:=c/b
        end square_equation;
    var a,b,c,x,y: REAL;
    exceptions
        when Wrong_data:
        writeln (t);
    begin
        read (a,b,c);
        square_equation(a,b,c,x,y);
        writeln (x,y);
    end
```

```
unit Knapsack_problem: procedure (A: arrayof INTEGER, volume: INTEGER);
  signal found;

    unit p: procedure (s,k: INTEGER);
      begin
        if s + A[k] > volume then return fi;
        if s + A[k] = volume then raise found fi;
        s := s + A[k];
        for i:=k + 1 to A.UPPER do p(s,i) od;
      lastwill : writeln (k);
      end p;

    exceptions
        when found : writeln (" sequence of indices:");
                      terminate

    begin
      for i:=A.LOWER to A.UPPER do p(0,i) od;
      writeln (" such a sequence does not exists");
    lastwill : writeln (" the end of sequence")
    end Knapsack_problem;
```

This procedure searches for a sequence of indices i1,i2,...,ik such that

A[i1]+A[i2]+...+A[ik]=volume,

assuming that A[i]>0 for all i and that A[i]>A[j] for i>j.

17.2. Exception Handling in Coroutines

Signals cannot be propagated by *raise statement* outside a coroutine. The transfer of information about exceptional events from one coroutine to another is possible due to the *exceptional coroutine statement*.

<exceptional coroutine statement> ::= <attach statement> **with**
<signal name> <actual parameter list>
References:
<attach statement> --> 15.2, <signal name> --> 17.1.2,
<actual parameter list> --> 9

The signal raised by *exceptional coroutine statement* must not have any *inout* or *output parameters*. After computation of signal's actual parameters, the control is transferred to the *resumed coroutine* according to the semantics of *attach statement* (see 15.2). Searching, activation and termination of the handler responding to the raised signal are performed as if that signal was raised at the point of the *coroutine resumption*.

Examples:

```
block unit tree: class; -- class representing a binary tree
                var left, right:tree;
                    val:INTEGER;
        end tree;

    unit traverse: coroutine (t:tree);
            var value:INTEGER;
 { consecutive elements of tree t are located repeatedly on "value"and sent to the
    attaching unit. }
            unit getn: procedure (node:tree); -- traverses the tree in the infix order
                begin
                  if node =/= none
                  then
                        getn(node.left);
                        value:=node.val;
                        attach (LAST_ATTACH)
                        getn(node.right)
                fi
            end getn;
          begin -- body of traverse
            return;     getn(t);
            attach (LAST_ATTACH) with end_of_tree(t)
        end traverse;
```

```
    signal end_of_tree(t:tree);
    var boo:BOOLEAN;   C1,C2,C:traverse;   T1,T2:tree;

  begin
{ program prints out the elements of two binarysearch trees T1 and T2 in the
  ascending order }
    { generation of T1 and T2 }
    boo:=FALSE;
    C1:=new traverse(T1);
    C2:=new traverse(T2);
    attach (C1);
    attach (C2);
    block -- traversing of two trees is multiplexed
        exceptions when end_of_tree:
            C:=C1;
            if t=T1 then C:=C2 fi;
            terminate
        end
      begin
        do C:=C1;
            if C1.value>C2.value then C:=C2 fi ;
            writeln (C.value);
            attach (C)
        od
    end;
    block -- only one tree remains to be traversed
        exceptions when end_of_tree: terminate
        begin do writeln (C.value);
                attach (C)
            od
    end
end
```

17.3. System Signals

Some of the signals, called system signals, are predefined in the language. They are raised automatically when a run−time error or another exceptional system situation appears.

System signals have no parameters. They are not declared in the signal specification, but the user may declare handlers for them. The execution of *return statement* is not allowed in the handler responding to such a signal.

The following signals are predefined in the language:

Acc_Error: Remote access via the reference to **none** .

Attach_Error: An attempt to *attach* an object of the *terminated coroutine* or an object which is not a *coroutine object.*

Comm_Error: An attempt to communicate by *alien* or *send* statement with not well-defined receiver.

Con_Error: The value of an index expression exceeds the range of *array indices* or *the array bounds* are incorrect, or value assigned to subtype variable is out of range.

Cor_Term : The signal raised when a *coroutine* is terminated.

Hand_Not_Found : An error terminating the execution of a process when a signal handler was not found.

Kill_Error: An attempt to kill a non-terminated object.

Mem_Error: A fatal error when there is no free space for the allocation of a new object.

Num_Error: A numerical error, such as for instance integer overflow, floating-point overflow, etc.

Sys_Error: Any kind of file system error like e.g. input-output error, parity error, etc.

Some other errors may also be introduced as system errors but they are not predefined in the language.

18. File Processing

18.1. File Categories

There are three categories of files:

- binary sequential file, identified by keyword **binary,**
- binary random file, identified by keyword **random,**
- text sequential file, identified by keyword **text.**

Binary sequential files and *binary random files* are sequences of components numbered by successive natural numbers, starting from zero. The component that will take part in the next i/o operation is called current component. The index of the current component is called current file position or shortly, file position. Any i/o operation increases current file position by the number of components which take part in the operation.

For *binary sequential files* the only way to affect the file position is to rewind a file (resetting the file position to zero) or to execute an i/o statement (advancing the file position). For *binary random files* it is possible to change the file position arbitrarily.

Text files are sequences of characters organized into lines. A line consists of any number of characters and ends with the end of line character.

A file declaration (see 4.4) specifies all possible types of components that may be saved in that file. The specified type must be a primitive (4.1), a discrete (4.2) or a composite (4.3) type built from these types. Moreover the following restrictions hold: enumeration types are allowed only in *binary sequential* and *binary random file declarations,* and string type is allowed only in a *text sequential file declaration.* Subtypes may be specified if and only if their base type may be specified. For *records, reference type* components are permitted, although they are never transmitted.

Although adjustable *array type* may not occur in the type specification of the file declaration, nevertheless, *adjustable arrays* can be read or written by an i/o operation provided that their component type appears in the *file type* specification (see 18.3.2).

18.2. Permanent and Scratch Files

A scratch (local) file exists only during a program execution. A permanent file exists in the operating system before and/or after a program execution.

To establish the association between a file variable and a permanent file existing in an operating system one of the two predefined procedures must be called:

– CREATE(f,s) creates a new permanent file,
– CONNECT(f,s) connects an existing file.

Parameter f designates a file variable, while parameter s is a string or a *static array* of type CHAR identifying a permanent file in the operating system.

The association of a file variable may be established only once and must be performed before the first i/o operation with this file variable. All file variables which are not associated with permanent files are associated with scratch files by default.

There are two predefined permanent files, identified "STANDARD INPUT" for input and "STANDARD OUTPUT" for *output operations*. As no declaration for these files appears in a program, all values of legal file component types may be saved on them. Both these predefined files are *text sequential.*

18.3. I/O Statements

<i/o statement>::= <text i/o statement> | <binary i/o statement>
References:
<text i/o statement> ––> 18.3.1
<binary i/o statement> ––> 18.3.2

18.3.1. Text I/O Statements

<text i/o statement>::= <read statement> | <write statement>
<read statement>::= {**read** | **readln** } {({<name>}? , <name list>) } | **readln**
<name list>::= {<name> ♯ , }+
<write statement>::= {**write** | **writeln** }
  {({{name>}? , <formatted expression list>})} |**writeln**
<formatted expression list>::=
  {<expression> { : <expression> }? {: <expression>}? ♯ , }+
References:
<name> ––> 6.1, <expression> ––> 6.2

The optional first name in the parameter list of *read* and *write statement*, if present, must designate a sequential file. If a predefined file is to be used, then this name may be omitted.

Each element of the formatted expression list is of the form E or E:E1 or E:E1:E2, where E designates a value to be written while E1 and E2 are static expressions specifying two integer constants c_1 and c_2, respectively. The values c_1 and c_2, if present, designate the format of the written value.

Let f denote a *text sequential file*, Xi (i=1,...,k) denote variables, and Pi (i=1,...k) denote formatted expressions.

Statement **read** (X1,...,Xk) is equivalent to statement **read** (f,X1,...,Xk) where f denotes the predefined input file. Statement **read** (f,X1,...,Xk) is equivalent to the sequence of statements **read** (f,X1); ...; **read** (f,Xk).

If X is of type CHAR, then **read** (f,X) reads one character from file f; if X is of numeric or boolean type the statement reads a sequence of characters which form (according to the syntax) a value of the type of variable X, the leading blanks are omitted.

If X is of a composite type, then statement **read** (f,X) is equivalent to the sequence of *read statements* for all components of the variable X, with the exception of components of a *reference type*.

If X is an *adjustable array*, then statement **read** (f,X) is equivalent to the appropriate sequence of *read statements* for all components of array X, unless these components are of *reference type*.

Statement **readln** (f,X1,...,Xk) is equivalent to the statements **read** (f,X1,...,Xk); **readln** (f). Statement **readln** (f) skips characters from the current line until the end of line is encountered; and then passes to a new line.

Statement **write** (P1,...,Pk) is equivalent to statement **write** (f,P1,...,Pk) where f denotes the predefined output file. Statement **write** (f,P1,...,Pk) is equivalent to the sequence of statements **write** (f,P1); ...; **write** (f,Pk).

If constants c_1, c_2 are omitted in a formatted expression, then the implementation defined values will be assumed. Constant c_1 specifies the width of the field for writing. The coded representation of written value will be right justified within the field of specified width. The meaning of constant c_2 depends on the type of the written value.

For any real type, numbers appear on output in the floating point representation with the standard exponential part, unless c_2 is used. In such a case c_2 determines the number of decimal digits that are written after the decimal point in the fixed point representation. For any boolean type c_2 determines the base of the representation. The default value of c_2 is 2, and only c_2 equal 2, 4, 8 or 16 is allowed. All other values of c_2 are ignored. For the remaining types, constant c_2 is ignored.

Write statement for composite type is equivalent to the sequence of *write statements* for all components of the value, with the exception of components of a *reference type*. Field width parameters for composite type value will be assumed for all components of that value.

Write statement for *adjustable array* is equivalent to the appropriate sequence of *write statements* for all components of an array, unless these components are of a *reference type*.

Statement **writeln** (f,P1,...,Pk) is equivalent to the statements **write** (f,P1,...,Pk); **writeln** (f). Statement **writeln** (f) terminates the current line and passes to a new line.

There are also two predefined operations that may be applied to a *text sequential file*:

EOF (f) — returns value TRUE if the end of file f is encountered, FALSE otherwise; this function may be called without any argument, and then it tests the end of the predefined input file (EOF).

SEEK (f,0) — procedure rewinding a file; for text sequential files the value of the second parameter must be equal zero.

The coded representation of the numeric or boolean literals in the input *text sequential files* must conform to the syntax rules for literals (see 2.5, 2.6). Moreover each representation of the value must be terminated by a delimiter or the end of line. None of the characters that can appear within the coded representation of the literal of the given type may be used as the delimiter.

18.3.2. Binary I/O Statements

<binary i/o statement>::= <get statement> | <put statement>
<get statement>::= **get** (<name> , <name list>)
<put statement>::= **put** (<name> , <expression list>)
References:
<name> --> 6.1, <name list> --> 18.3.1
<expression list> --> 6.1.2

For *binary sequential* and *binary random files* each operation refers to the entire component. It means that any file component must be written or read by a single i/o statement.

There are following i/o statements for *binary* and *random files*:

> **get** (f,X1,...,Xk) – reads from file f and assigns read values to the given variables X1,...,Xk,

> **put** (f,E1,...,Ek) – writes on file f the values defined by the expressions E1,...,Ek.

Similarly as for *text i/o statements* the *put* or *get statements* with a sequence of arguments are equivalent to the sequences of statements with two arguments. The transmission of composite type values is performed analogously.

There are also three predefined operations that may be applied to *binary sequential* or *binary random files*:

> POSITION(f) — integer function which returns the number of a current file position;

> SEEK(f,n) — for random files assigns a current file position to n; for sequential files rewinds a file if n=0, otherwise Sys_Error is raised;

> EOF (f) — returns value TRUE if the end of file is achieved, FALSE otherwise; for random files it means that the value of the current file position is greater than the greatest index of a saved component.

Examples:

As it was mentioned before, *adjustable array type* may not occur in a file declaration, but an *adjustable array* can be saved on a file. It can be done as follows:

> **type** afile : **random** fileof REAL;
> **var** A : **arrayof** REAL;
>   f : afile;   { f is a scratch file }
>   n : INTEGER;
>   ...
> **read** (n);   { reads from the predefined input file }
> A := **new array** [1..n];
>   ...
> **put** (f,A);

The statement **put** (f,A) where A is an *adjustable array* is equivalent to the statement:

> **if** A =/= **none then**
>   **for** i:=A.LOWER **to** A.UPPER **do put** (f,A[i]) **od**
> **fi**

18.4. Termination of File Processing

There are two predefined procedures that break the association between a file variable and a permanent file:

> DISCONNECT(f) — saves the permanent file associated with file variable f in the operating system,

> DELETE(f) — removes the permanent file associated with file variable f from the operating system.

These two procedures can be applied to scratch files with no effect to the operating system. After the execution of any of these operations file f is empty and it is in the same state as before file association. In particular, it means that file variable f may be associated to another permanent file.

19. Bibliography

[1] Banachowski L., Kreczmar A., Mirkowska G., Rasiowa H., Salwicki A.: An Introduction to Algorithmic Logic. Mathematical Investigations in the Theory of Programs. *In Banach Center Publications*, Warsaw 1977.

[2] Bartol W.M, Kreczmar A., Litwiniuk A., Oktaba H.: Semantics and Implementation of Prefixing at Many Levels, *Proceedings of Conference: Logic of Programs and Their Applications, Springer LNCS 148, pp.45-80,* 1983.

[3] Bobrow D.G., Common Loops: Merging Common Lisp and Object Oriented Programming, *ACM-SIGPLAN Notices, Vol.21, No.1, pp.17-29,* 1986

[4] Cioni G., Kreczmar A.: Programmed Deallocation Without Dangling Reference, *IPL 18, pp.179-187,* 1984.

[5] Dahl O-J., Myhrhaug B., Nygaard K.: Common Base Language. *NCC s-22, October,* Oslo 1970.

[6] Dahl O-J., Wang A.: Coroutine Sequencing in a Block Structured Environment. *BIT Vol.11, pp.425-49,* 1971.

[7] Feldman J.A., High Level Programming for Distributed Computing, *CACM, Vol.22, No.6, pp.353-368,* 1979.

[8] Hansen P.B.: Concurrent Pascal, a Programming Language for Operating System Design, *IST Report No.10,* 1974.

[9] Hoare C.A.R.: Monitors, an Operating System Structuring Concept. *CACM, Vol.17, No.10, pp.549-557,* 1974.

[10] Ingalls D., The Smalltalk 76 Programming System Design and Implementation, *Proceedings of the Fifth POPL Conference, pp.9-16,* 1978.

[11] Krause M., Kreczmar A., Langmaack H., Salwicki A., Specification and Implementation Problems of Programming Languages Proper for Hierarchical Data Types, *Bericht. Inst. Informatik Univ. Kiel 8410,* Kiel 1984.

[12] Krause M., Langmaack H., Kreczmar A., Warpechowski M., Concatenation of Program Modules, an Algebraic Approach to the Semantic and Implementation Problems. *Proceedings of Conference : Computation Theory, Springer LNCS 208, pp.134-156,* 1986.

[13] Moon D., Object Oriented Programming with Flavors, *ACM-SIGPLAN Notices, Vol.21, No.1, pp.1-8,* 1986

[14] Müldner T.: On the Semantics of Parallel Programs. *ICS PAS Report 348*, Warsaw 1979.

[15] Myhre O.: Protecting Attributes of a Local Class. *SIMULA Newsletters, Vol.5, No.4*, 1977.

[16] Naur P.(ed): Revised Report on the Algorithmic Language ALGOL 60. *ACM Vol.6, pp.1-7*, 1963.

[17] Preliminary ADA Reference Manual. *Sigplan Notices, Vol.14, No.6*, 1979.

[18] Wirth N.: The Programming Language PASCAL, *Acta Informatica, Vol.1, pp.35-63*, 1971.

[19] Salwicki A.: Formalized Algorithmic Languages, *Bull.Acad.Polon.Sci. No.18, pp.227-232*, 1970.

[20] Salwicki A.: Applied Algorithmic Logic. *Proc. of MFCS'77. Springer LNCS Vol.53, pp.122-134*, 1977.

[21] Sherman M., Paragon,*Springer LNCS Vol.189*, 1982

[22] Stroustrup B., An Overview of C++, *SIGPLAN Notices, Vol.21, No.11, pp.7-18*, 1986

[23] Bruun Kristensen B., Lehrmann Madsen O., Möller–Pedersen B., Nygaard K.: The BETA Programming Language, Aarhus Univ., DAIMI PB – 229, Nov. 1987.

[24] Krause M.: Die Korrektheit einer Implementation der Modulpräfigierung mit reiner Static-Scope-Semantik, Inst. Informatik Prakt. Math. Univ. Kiel, 8616, 1986.

[25] Krogdahl S.: On the Implementation of BETA, Norwegian Comp. Centre, 1979.

20. Index

Vol. 379: A. Kreczmar, G. Mirkowska (Eds.), Mathematical Foundations of Computer Science 1989. Proceedings, 1989. VIII, 605 pages. 1989.

Vol. 380: J. Csirik, J. Demetrovics, F. Gécseg (Eds.), Fundamentals of Computation Theory. Proceedings, 1989. XI, 493 pages. 1989.

Vol. 381: J. Dassow, J. Kelemen (Eds.), Machines, Languages, and Complexity. Proceedings, 1988. VI, 244 pages. 1989.

Vol. 382: F. Dehne, J.-R. Sack, N. Santoro (Eds.), Algorithms and Data Structures. WADS '89. Proceedings, 1989. IX, 592 pages. 1989.

Vol. 383: K. Furukawa, H. Tanaka, T. Fujisaki (Eds.), Logic Programming '88. Proceedings, 1988. VII, 251 pages. 1989 (Subseries LNAI).

Vol. 384: G. A. van Zee, J. G. G. van de Vorst (Eds.), Parallel Computing 1988. Proceedings, 1988. V, 135 pages. 1989.

Vol. 385: E. Börger, H. Kleine Büning, M.'M. Richter (Eds.), CSL '88. Proceedings, 1988. VI, 399 pages. 1989.

Vol. 386: J.E. Pin (Ed.), Formal Properties of Finite Automata and Applications. Proceedings, 1988. VIII, 260 pages. 1989.

Vol. 387: C. Ghezzi, J. A. McDermid (Eds.), ESEC '89. 2nd European Software Engineering Conference. Proceedings, 1989. VI, 496 pages. 1989.

Vol. 388: G. Cohen, J. Wolfmann (Eds.), Coding Theory and Applications. Proceedings, 1988. IX, 329 pages. 1989.

Vol. 389: D.H. Pitt, D. E. Rydeheard, P. Dybjer, A.M. Pitts, A. Poigné (Eds.), Category Theory and Computer Science. Proceedings, 1989. VI, 365 pages. 1989.

Vol. 390: J.P. Martins, E.M. Morgado (Eds.), EPIA 89. Proceedings, 1989. XII, 400 pages. 1989 (Subseries LNAI).

Vol. 391: J.-D. Boissonnat, J.-P. Laumond (Eds.), Geometry and Robotics. Proceedings, 1988. VI, 413 pages. 1989.

Vol. 392: J.-C. Bermond, M. Raynal (Eds.), Distributed Algorithms. Proceedings, 1989. VI, 315 pages. 1989.

Vol. 393: H. Ehrig, H. Herrlich, H.-J. Kreowski, G. Preuß (Eds.), Categorical Methods in Computer Science. VI, 350 pages. 1989.

Vol. 394: M. Wirsing, J.A. Bergstra (Eds.), Algebraic Methods: Theory, Tools and Applications. VI, 558 pages. 1989.

Vol. 395: M. Schmidt-Schauß, Computational Aspects of an Order-Sorted Logic with Term Declarations. VIII, 171 pages. 1989. (Subseries LNAI).

Vol. 396: T.A. Berson, T. Beth (Eds.), Local Area Network Security. Proceedings, 1989. IX, 152 pages. 1989.

Vol. 397: K.P. Jantke (Ed.), Analogical and Inductive Inference. Proceedings, 1989. IX, 338 pages. 1989. (Subseries LNAI).

Vol. 398: B. Banieqbal, H. Barringer, A. Pnueli (Eds.), Temporal Logic in Specification. Proceedings, 1987. VI, 448 pages. 1989.

Vol. 399: V. Cantoni, R. Creutzburg, S. Levialdi, G. Wolf (Eds.), Recent Issues in Pattern Analysis and Recognition. VII, 400 pages. 1989.

Vol. 400: R. Klein, Concrete and Abstract Voronoi Diagrams. IV, 167 pages. 1989.

Vol. 401: H. Djidjev (Ed.), Optimal Algorithms. Proceedings, 1989. VI, 308 pages. 1989.

Vol. 402: T. P. Bagchi, V. K. Chaudhri, Interactive Relational Database Design. XI, 186 pages. 1989.

Vol. 403: S. Goldwasser (Ed.), Advances in Cryptology – CRYPTO '88. Proceedings, 1988. XI, 591 pages. 1990.

Vol. 404: J. Beer, Concepts, Design, and Performance Analysis of a Parallel Prolog Machine. VI, 128 pages. 1989.

Vol. 405: C. E. Veni Madhavan (Ed.), Foundations of Software Technology and Theoretical Computer Science. Proceedings, 1989. VIII, 339 pages. 1989.

Vol. 407: J. Sifakis (Ed.), Automatic Verification Methods for Finite State Systems. Proceedings, 1989. VII, 382 pages. 1990.

Vol. 408: M. Leeser, G. Brown (Eds.) Hardware Specification, Verification and Synthesis: Mathematical Aspects. Proceedings, 1989. VI, 402 pages. 1990.

Vol. 409: A. Buchmann, O. Günther, T. R. Smith, Y.-F. Wang (Eds.), Design and Implementation of Large Spatial Databases. Proceedings, 1989. IX, 364 pages. 1990.

Vol. 410: F. Pichler, R. Moreno-Diaz (Eds.), Computer Aided Systems Theory – EUROCAST '89. Proceedings, 1989. VII, 427 pages. 1990.

Vol. 411: M. Nagl (Ed.), Graph-Theoretic Concepts in Computer Science. Proceedings, 1989. VII, 374 pages. 1990.

Vol. 412: L. B. Almeida, C. J. Wellekens (Eds.), Neural Networks. Proceedings, 1990. IX, 276 pages. 1990.

Vol. 413: R. Lenz, Group Theoretical Methods in Image Processing. VIII, 139 pages. 1990.

Vol. 414: A. Kreczmar, A. Salwicki, M. Warpechowski, LOGLAN '88 – Report on the Programming Language. X, 133 pages. 1990.